797,885 Books

are available to read at

Forgotten Books

www.ForgottenBooks.com

Forgotten Books' App
Available for mobile, tablet & eReader

Download on the
App Store

ANDROID APP ON
Google play

ISBN 978-1-330-55729-7
PIBN 10078300

This book is a reproduction of an important historical work. Forgotten Books uses
state-of-the-art technology to digitally reconstruct the work, preserving the original format
whilst repairing imperfections present in the aged copy. In rare cases, an imperfection in
the original, such as a blemish or missing page, may be replicated in our edition. We do,
however, repair the vast majority of imperfections successfully; any imperfections that
remain are intentionally left to preserve the state of such historical works.

Forgotten Books is a registered trademark of FB &c Ltd.
Copyright © 2015 FB &c Ltd.
FB &c Ltd, Dalton House, 60 Windsor Avenue, London, SW19 2RR.
Company number 08720141. Registered in England and Wales.

For support please visit www.forgottenbooks.com

1 MONTH OF
FREE
READING

at

www.ForgottenBooks.com

By purchasing this book you are eligible for one month membership to ForgottenBooks.com, giving you unlimited access to our entire collection of over 700,000 titles via our web site and mobile apps.

To claim your free month visit:
www.forgottenbooks.com/free78300

* Offer is valid for 45 days from date of purchase. Terms and conditions apply.

Similar Books Are Available from
www.forgottenbooks.com

The Life of the Spirit and the Life of Today
by Evelyn Underhill

The Key to the Universe
by Harriette Augusta Curtiss

Optimism
The Lesson of Ages, by Benjamin Paul Blood

Spiritual Science
by Oliver Loraine Wroughton

In the Hours of Meditation
by A Disciple

The Inner Consciousness
How to Awaken and Direct It, by Swami Prakashananda

Spiritual Healing
by William Frederick Cobb

The Nature of Spirit, and of Man As a Spiritual Being
by Chauncey Giles

This Mystical Life of Ours
by Ralph Waldo Trine

Self-Knowledge and Self-Discipline
by B. W. Maturin

The Subconscious Mind and Its Illuminating Light
by Janet Young

The Pathway of Roses
by Christian D. Larson

The Hygiene of the Soul
Memoir of a Physician and Philosopher, by Gustav Pollak

The Smile
If You Can Do Nothing Else, You Can Smile, by S. S. Curry

Spiritual Reading for Every Day, Vol. 1 of 2
An Introduction to the Interior and Perfect Life, by Kenelm Digby Best

Vedanta Philosophy
Three Lectures on Spiritual Unfoldment, by Swâmi Abhedânanda

Angel Voices from the Spirit World
Glory to God Who Sends Them, by James Lawrence

Spiritual Director and Physician
The Spiritual Treatment of Sufferers from Nerves and Scruples, by Viktor Raymond

The Ten Commandments
An Interpretation, or the Constitution of the Spiritual Universe, by George Chainey

Cosmic Consciousness
The Man-God Whom We Await, by Ali Nomad

THE SMALL END

OF

GREAT PROBLEMS

By
BROOKE HERFORD, D.D.

Sermons of Courage and Cheer
Post 8vo

The Story of Religion in England
Post 8vo

THE SMALL END

of

GREAT PROBLEMS

BY

BROOKE HERFORD, D.D.

LATE MINISTER OF ROSSLYN HILL CHAPEL
LONDON
SOMETIME PREACHER TO HARVARD
UNIVERSITY, U. S. A.

LIBRARY
JUN 2
THEOLOGICAL

LONGMANS, GREEN, AND CO.

91 and 93 FIFTH AVENUE, NEW YORK
LONDON AND BOMBAY
1902

Copyright, 1902, by

LONGMANS, GREEN, AND CO.

—————

All rights reserved

LANGUAGES PRINTING COMPANY, NEW YORK, U.S.A.

CONTENTS

THE SMALL END OF GREAT PROBLEMS

My thought is one for the simplifying of the problems and perplexities of life. You know what these are: — problems of duty; problems of religion; problems of Nature and of life — of what Life is, and what it is for, and of what is going to be the end of it; problems of man and of God — of time and of eternity. Gradually, this idea has shaped itself out to me — of how much the problems and perplexities of life would be simplified if people would only take hold of them at the small end.

You see we stand at a sort of centre. Each life is central to the whole universe. From each little centre of your or my life, the Universe stretches away infinitely. Things seem pretty plain just where we are, but as they stretch away into the distance they lose themselves in an horizon of mystery. And even that horizon is not the end, but suggests infinite distances beyond, entirely out of our ken. Our outlook is like the wedge-shaped track of light cast from a lantern into the darkness. It is small, but very bright close to, then as it widens out it becomes constantly dimmer, and at last it is wholly lost.

It is perfectly true that the same laws hold good, the same truths are true from the centre to the circumference; but it is one thing to be sure that the same law and truth are there, away at the infinite end of things out of sight, and quite another to be able to see how the law and truth apply there.

For instance — take gravitation. I can make out something of what gravitation means, close here, as it works in what we call " weight " and in the forces which cause things to stand or fall. But when I follow it out and try to realise what gravitation means between stars millions of millions of miles apart, my mind gets dazed; and when I follow it out further yet, into the abstract question of what gravitation is, and how it is related to the absolute cause and force of this vast universe, then my mind is simply lost, I cannot even form an idea about that. Well, my point is, that if you want to get any real practical hold of this idea of gravitation, you must study it first at the smaller end of it, close about us.

You will see the value of keeping this clearly in view when you remember that strange as it may seem, this is not the natural way. The near and the simple are the last things that affect the mind. Man is constantly wanting to begin at the big end of things and of thoughts. In the beginning of knowledge, man's mind is confident and wants to spread itself. The child thinks it could manage the household very well. The raw recruit would willingly undertake to be General. If you have any literary gift, you are apt to feel as if you could write a book that should at once be a success. When I first started to preach, I had a profound conviction that if I could only get a fair hearing I could convert the human race. At twenty-one, one would undertake to run the Universe. We want to spread ourselves on the large circumference of things. So in Art. Simplicity is not the first grace of Art, but the last and finest perfection of it. The savage pays small attention to the flower at his feet, but gazes with intensity of wonder on the lightning flash or the comet. And it is not only youth and savagism that think in this inverted order. Philosophy began at the large end of its problems — with large general speculations. Thales would have it that water was the fundamental essence of the universe; Anaximenes found it in air; Pythagoras sought it in the mystic relations of numbers. They began with such faraway generalizations, and only quite gradually worked down to the close facts of nature. Also with the old theologians. They were always constructing vast theories of abstract Divinity, but had little eye for what God is actually doing, here and now.

So the true order of thinking and living needs continually emphasizing — from the small to the great, from the near to the far, from the known to the unknown, from fact to theory, from sight to faith: study and attempt the prob lems of life from the small, near end of them.

In some realms of inquiry, in some of the directions of man's restless thought, we have come to a pretty clear understanding of this principle. It is so in Science for instance. That is what makes the science of the present day such a noble and useful thing. The science of the ancients did not amount to much, not because it had not got far enough — it had got further than many people are aware — but because it began at the wrong end. It began with those ideas of some vague universal essence — air, water, numbers, — and worked down from those far off theories to the facts of nature close at hand; and of course it made a pretty poor mess of the facts. Now the science of the present day is so hopeful because it grapples with the mystery of Nature at its small, near end. It begins with the palpable facts close about us. Newton studies the falling apple and comes nearer the explanation of the solar system, than any one had ever done before. Franklin draws down a little lightning to his own knuckles, and observes it there. When Darwin wants to find out how things have come to be, he sets to work to see how they are coming and becoming now. A thousand careful observers are watching the tiny facts of plant and insect, of rock and shell; the exact fall of rain, the precise direction and force of the wind currents. Nothing is too common or too small. The roadside pebble, the lump of coal, the seed-vessel of a dandelion, the chemistry of a rain drop — there is nothing more beautiful than the way in which modern science teaches men respect for, and interest in the tiny fact close at their feet. When Science has also learned that the thought and feeling in a man's heart is as much a fact, a reality, as the stone at his feet, then shall we be in about as fair a way as we can be — I do not say for actually solving the problem of Being, but for solving as much of it as is within man's scope at all.

In morals too — questions of right and duty — the modern world is becoming familiar with this principle of taking hold of problems by their small near end. I think that 'this is largely due to Christianity. For, if you look into it, you will see that this is the very spirit of Christ, both in regard to the simplest matters of doing right and the most complicated problems of Christian thought. Christ did not indeed speak of " problems " or of taking hold of them at this nearer end. But he was always doing it, and teaching men to do it. The beginning of the Kingdom of God, he shews is as small as a mustard seed. The place to grapple with sin, is not at the circumference of action, but at the centre of thought. It had been said by them of old time " Thou shalt not kill." Christ puts it — " You must take hold of that matter at a smaller end than that — you must not even be angry." The angry feeling he puts as the smaller end of the murderous deed. So with all moral questions. Christ brought the right and wrong of things down from the clouds to the earth, from the traditions of the Rabbis to the common sense of the common people. They were working out their Sabbath law by abstract theorising from some supposed Divine Will in the beginning of Creation, — " The

Sabbath was made for man," said Jesus, and brought the question down to what is good for you and me to-day. So, that golden summing up of duty — " Whatsoever ye would that men should do to you, do ye even so to them " — that was not a maxim of mutual axe-grinding, but the bringing of the great problem of righteousness to its smallest end, just where it touches me and my neighbour. And so of deeper questions. Some one asked him " Lord, are there few that be saved? " Why, that was just one of those problems which at the larger end cover the whole vista of Eternity. But Christ would not even touch it at that larger end. Simply — " Strive thou to enter in at the strait gate " — just the small personal end of that great problem. And what a helpful saying that is for those who are perplexing themselves over large abstract religious questions — " If a man will do God's will, he shall know of the doctrine." Do the best you can — just *do* that; begin with the small near thing where you can see it, and the way will clear, the larger principle or doctrine will open out to you.

There is the marvellous thing in Christ — his mighty opening of man's thought to the Divine surroundings and infinities of life — while yet constantly bringing men down to the common

things close about them as the way to that
Divine. Often men would like to stay up in
the cloudlands of Divine mystery — but Christianity won't let them. It keeps bringing them
back to the work and the neighbour and the
little child. Christianity is doing this to-day.
It is just this which is making society impatient
of mere abstruse creeds, which is making the
churches crave less of the Apocalypse and more
of the Sermon on the Mount; and which so is
making them less divided in their interpretations
of the Heavenly Mysteries and more united in
trying at this nearer end of things to make this
common world a more wholesome, honest, and
happier place.

And yet, clear as this principle stands in Christianity, there are plenty of moral questions in
which men still confuse themselves, just for lack
of it! Take for instance the small deceits and
sharp practices of trade — I do not mean the
great criminal dishonesties, but the small de-
ceptions and over-reachings which no law can
punish and yet which will not stand the light.
How do *good* men persuade themselves into doing these questionable things? Not how do bad
men do them, no difficulty about that, but how
do good men do them? Well, you will find
that it is very much by looking at the larger

end of the problem. They take the large numerical aspect of it; they say to themselves " everybody does these things — here is the universal custom — we did not make it, and we cannot alter it." You see, by looking at the little half-penny dishonesty at the big end, it comes to seem almost respectable, like a sort of unalterable law of nature!

So it is with numbers of moral problems. Look at them at the large end, as vast abstract problems, and you will be very apt to get confused; but look at them at the small near end, as simple questions of truth and right between yourself and those you are concerned with — and — I do not say you will always find it easy to do the right thing, but at any rate you will not often be in much doubt as to what the right thing is.

The same principle would often help us in solving the problems of the larger life, of peoples. How many of the high flying social theories by which enthusiasts would regenerate the world, collapse the moment you take hold of them and try them, at their smaller end. What a fine thing Communism appears, at the big end of it — all the good things of the world divided fairly among all — plenty, surely, for everybody. Do you wonder that men, sad at the want and woe of earth have dreamed of Communism as the remedy? But look at it at the smaller end — what it would really mean to the individual. I am afraid it would not be much more than it brought to that Communistic workman, who in a stage coach in Germany — having no idea who the passenger in the corner was — began to denounce Baron Rothschild, with his forty million thalers of property. "What right has he to all that" he said; "it is robbery, it belongs to the people!"

By and bye Rothschild looked up from his corner and said: — "How many people are there in Germany?"

Someone supplied the information that there were about forty millions. "Well, well," said the old Banker, "then that is just a thaler apiece. Here, my good friend," he continued, pulling out his purse: "I am Rothschild, and here is your thaler. Now you are settled with." Yes, a few thalers apiece and a great deal less of stimulus and scope for personal effort — I am afraid that would be all of it, at the smaller end.

Or do you want to know how equality is suited to human beings? Study it in the nursery or the playground. Said Lycurgus to one who advised that a democracy should be set up in Sparta — " My friend, try a democracy in your own house!"

In fact, is not the real solution of all the great problems of National life, just at this smaller end? The problem of good government has to be solved in the ward meeting The man must be grappled with in the child. When the Duke of Wellington saw the Eton boys playing football, as if their lives depended on it, he said " That is where the battle of Waterloo was won!" The witty Frenchman went further back still, and said " If you want to reform a man, you must begin with his Grandmother." But seriously, is it not the case that almost all the problems of national well-being have their solution in some smaller matter of personal faithfulness and right-doing? That is a good proverb the Chinese have, which somebody has rendered into the little rhyme:—

> " If every one would see,
>   To his own reformation,
>   How very easily,
>   You might reform a nation!"

The same with Institutions. Do you want to start some movement that shall live and grow? Be content to begin small. For my part I am always distrustful of an institution that begins large with a fine building, a great staff of officials and so forth.   I have sometimes thought that the difference between the Priest and Levite — and — the Good Samaritan, may not have been that the Priest and Levite were so much more hard-hearted but only that they were the kind of people who do not care to grapple with the problem of doing good unless they can take hold of the large end of it and do a great lump of good all at once.   I can imagine that that priest may have gone home and told his family what a sad sight he had seen — a poor man robbed and half murdered lying by the roadside — such a sad sight indeed, that he really could not trust himself to go any nearer .   .   . and that it had made him feel that there ought to be a society started to deal with such cases, which had been sadly too common on that Jericho road; and that he would speak to High-priest Caiaphas about it and get him to be president and some of the leading Scribes and Pharisees to go on the Committee, and they would have a regular patrol staff with proper ambulances.

But meanwhile what of the poor wounded man? Fortunately for him, there came the Samaritan by that way — and he was one who believed in taking hold of the problem of human

suffering by the small end — which meant helping that poor fellow lying there — giving him
some of the oil and wine out of his own lunch-
basket and setting him on his own beast even
though he himself had to walk. That is the
true principle in Philanthropy. We want more
Individualism, less Institutionalism. The sins
and troubles of the world are not going to be
reached en masse. It has mostly to be one by
one, heart and soul work. No stateliest asylum
is so good, either for the orphans or even (they
are finding out) for the blind or the deaf, as
life even in the poorest homes. Be sure it is
a needed thing you have in view and then never
be afraid to begin small. It does not follow
you are to stay small! I believe in a large en-
terprising spirit, but, take hold of these practical
problems by the small end.

I think that this principle has its most deeply
helpful application to the great problems of
thought, and it is for these that I am really
speaking of it. These problems of God, and
Man, and the Dim Future — why, the minds
of men are aching to-day with their craving to
get to some clear strong resting place, something
that they can feel sure of.

Sometimes in despair, they try to give up
thinking and not trouble themselves. But they

cannot. The old thoughts come back, the old
questions, the old mysteries. It is one of the
signs of man's higher nature — this inability to
rest in the near and the actual and the outward.
Only, let our thinking begin with these — that
is my point — and then it will at least have a
chance of coming to something.

Why, take the greatest problem of all — that
of the Being of God. I can only glance at it,
for my object is not to work out full answers on
these subjects, but to show which way some
answer lies. And I take this as one of those
deep solemn mysteries which in all ages have
set man's brain throbbing and aching in the endeavour to grasp it. What does it mean, to say
" God? " Think of all these infinite worlds, that
Milky Way with its flush of light across the sky
— just a sort of sand-dust of worlds, too far
off for any figures to tell. Can you think of
an Infinite Mind, present throughout those
awful world spaces, and age upon age, through
countless cycles of eternity — still, God — God
— unchanged, the same? Why, when one tries
even to look at that large far away end of the
problem, one's mind only grows dizzy. Often,
when I have tried to think it out, so, I have felt
as if I could not believe anything. But, come
to the nearer end. I go into the fields in the

summer time.   I take up a wild flower, or the folded leaf just bursting from its bud sheath — and somehow I cannot help feeling " That did not make itself; something meant that."   I cannot resist that flower.   It speaks to me, close to, of wisdom, purpose, beneficent will.   I look thus at the smaller end of the great problem, and I cannot help believing.

Or take the problem of Man.   What is man? What can he do?   Can man do anything?   Has he really any will, or free choice of his own? Look at that question at its larger end as an abstract philosophical problem — and you get lost directly.   Start from that far off abstraction — in itself quite indisputable — that God must be omniscient, and it seems quite clear: therefore He must know all that man will do, and therefore man can only do that, cannot have any real choice or will.   Or start with that large consideration of Law; Law everywhere, in everything — so that not a grain of sand can get out of its place in this vast universe, and try how that will fit with the idea of there being as many free wills as there are human beings — a thousand million wills, separate, distinct, each going its own way.   It seems absurd.   No! At that larger end of things, I cannot fit in human freedom, either with God's Omniscient

Will or nature's all-embracing law.   But bring your thought down to the smaller end, of your own personal surroundings and feelings, and you can — only — fit freedom in with these.

Here is your breakfast here is your work. Consider that not a single meal or a single day can be creditably got through without your assuming that you have real power of choice, and recognise that this universe is not run on shams and make-believes — and, here, at the small near end of that free-will problem, it is plain enough. There is no real doubt.   You are not a mere pair of scales, that have to go up or down just as the heaviest motives are put in here or there.   You are a person, who holds the scales and weighs motives, and then decides.   The world, on the larger view may look automatic, but at the small end of your own place and part in it, you know that you are not an automaton.

And it is the same with the problem of all this struggling, sorrowing, tempted, sinning, multitudinous human life, away in the infinite beyond. Have you ever realised how that problem of human destiny has pressed on the thinkers of man-kind and what curious answers they have sometimes worked out to it?

In the Harvard University Library and in the British Museum, there is a little treatise by

Dr. Lewis Du Moulin, a learned Oxford Pro-
fessor, some 200 years ago. This is the title of
it : —

"Moral Reflections upon the number of the
"elect — proving plainly from Scripture evi-
"dence that not one in a hundred thousand, nay
"probably not one in a million, from Adam
"down to our times, shall be saved." Think of
it — not one in a hundred thousand saved, that
certainly, probably not one in a million. Now
how did a good thoughtful man manage to reason himself into such a confusion, which makes
us shudder to-day? By taking hold of the problem at the large far-away end of it. He started
with some vast far off idea of Divine decrees —
and reasoning back, by the time he got down
to man, he could hardly find any logically saved.
Well — how are we to answer such arguments?
Are we to go off with them into that vague, vast
region of abstract thought and try to refute
them there? No! Take hold of the problem
here at the near, human end of it. All these
men, women and children about us, take them
as they are; none altogether good, none altogether bad; has the dear Lord who made them
nothing in store for them but endless woe, for
all but one in a hundred thousand? Somehow
the moment we look at the problem at this nearer

end, it begins to grow a little clearer, a little more hopeful.

Indeed Christ's whole teaching of God as a heavenly father is a putting of the subject of God's purposes at its smaller end. By our own love for our children we can reach out towards the larger end of the great problem, and find — not indeed knowledge, but a happy trust as to what will somehow be done by that infinite life which " fathers and mothers " this great Universe of Being. I do not think even John Calvin himself could have made out quite such a grim theology if he had studied those divine decrees from this end of them, with the name Heavenly Father in his mind and a little child nestling in his arms.

The practical wisdom of all this is here: we are finite beings, surrounded by infinity and every line of action, observation, thought, along which we try to work or look, soon edges off to heights and depths which our working cannot attain, nor our thinking fathom. Yet close about us it is light. A little circle is within our reach. Here is this mighty earth, and for the life of us we cannot tell what it really is, or what a grain of it is, but we know how to use it. Here is our own life and we do not know what life is — but we know what living is, and how we may live just here to-day so as to find good and blessing. Here are all our fellow creatures, and they suggest a hundred problems of being and destiny in which any one may — in about ten minutes — lose himself in endless doubt; — but — these fellow creatures are real enough — their powers, their characters, sorrows, joys, and varied interests as they weave in with our living, there is no indistinctness about these. — Well, here is our dominion. Within this little circle close to us let us live the best and most we can — and from this centre feel out our way towards the larger relations and the infinite life. Begin at the small end — it is the true way both in practical things and in theoretical. Even in all the solemn infinite mystery of life, do not turn away from it, do not try to ignore it as hopelessly out of reach. Only, in looking that way and thinking that way, keep a firm foot on the solid earth and a close grip of your brother's hand. Reverence the near close facts of things as they appear to your natural eye and your common sense. That is the way to the highest thought and truth. Those highest things — Being, God and Destiny — are not out of our ken if we will feel our way towards them with this clue of believing that

the near and human things are parts of the
Divine, and indications of the Divine.   Then
will our very recognition of all that is best in
man oblige us to believe in God, and the present
life will lead us by its deepest qualities and possibilities to faith in a still greater future.   So
comes that living, confident faith which the
world is longing for to-day — a faith not sus-
pended as it were from some dim authority of
ancient texts but a faith rooted in the common
need and longing of mankind; a faith climbing
upwards through plant and star, and through
the little child and the grown man, and through
the long growth of the Bible, and the perfect
outcome of Christ — through all this, climbing
upward to the Infinite Fatherhood and the eternal life of Heaven.   So faith grows out of fact,
and in the growing ever verifies itself, and
throws back on the fact an ever nobler meaning; and thought widens and life grows larger,
and the world of man moves onwards — not yet
into any clear knowledge, indeed, — but surely
towards it; towards it, enough to make us sure
that our faith is not a baseless dream, but a
true light that lightens towards the Infinite
and the Divine.

THE UNSEEN THINGS THE MOST REAL

To SOME people this seems like reversing the true order of things. To look at things which cannot be seen, seems to them rather a waste of time. "Surely," they say, "we had better look at what can be seen!" Then, to talk of those unseen things as the "eternal" things, the most absolutely and enduringly real — seems a dreamy assertion about something which nobody can really know. Yes, I know that is how it is apt to seem to those who want to keep to "facts" and to "things which can be proved." Yet it is not really so; and I want our thoughts to rise above this tyranny of the seen — this impression of there being something especially real in things that we can see and handle. Whereas, when we consider the matter at all deeply, it is really exactly the other way. In putting it thus, I am not referring just to the soul and God. Those later, if you will. But the helpful thing, in thinking towards those higher unseen things, is to look right down on

the earth, among the common things that are
palpable to everyone, and to find that it is in
these first of all that the truth comes out —
that it is not anything we see that is most real
and lasting, but the unseen in them.   Only, perhaps when we find this so, even among the earth's
common visible things, it may help us to follow
the same truth a little more confidently, in its
higher relations to man and immortality and
God.

Well, look how it is among these common,
visible substances of the world; earth, water,
plant, animal, vegetable fibre, animal tissue —
now, are these eternal? or, do not let us use the
word " eternal." That seems to be carrying
the question too far.   Let us use the word lasting or permanent, which only carries the
thought as far as we can track it.   Put it, then
— are these things, earth, water, plant, animal,
and so forth — permanent?   Something   in
them is — but — precisely not that which you
see.   That which you see is constantly changing.   The face of the world, the world of things
that you see, is never quite the same, even for
two days.   Every leaf is changing, and in a
little while, as a leaf, as that which you see, it
is gone.   The solid lump of coal vanishes into
flame and smoke, which you only see for a mo-

ment, and into gas which you cannot see at all. The massive stone you build with, is eaten away by invisible chemicals in the air, and slowly decays. What do we mean by "decays?" Every word we use of that kind is really an affirmation of this very thought of Paul's, of something unseen which is what really endures. You say: the coal, the solid building stone, are not destroyed, they still exist in other forms. True, but your saying so only helps my showing — and even leads it, at once, to its higher bearings — for what is it that follows these curious processes, and tracks them out? What is it in you and me which traces the coal, on, into the gas, and the stone into invisible chemical elements? Something in you and me, also, which is invisible — not this mere hand, or this mere eye — something invisible in us. Anyhow — the seen things, the visible substance, is but for a time. That which endures is, certain invisible elements in these seen things and, in my visible body, an invisible intelligence that follows these invisible elements and feels that they are the lasting realities.

And the further you pursue these investigations of the visible things of the world, the more curiously true you find this. Why, instead of that which you see of anything, or in anything, being the great lasting reality, it is only a mere starting point. That which you see is only of any consequence, indeed as an indication of things which you cannot see. What is science? " Science " is the name we give to what we consider the most certain kind of knowledge. When a man says " this or that is a fact of science " he means to emphasize its certainty — that it is not a mere supposition, but something there is no mistake or doubt about. And yet see — " Science " hardly begins till you have got beyond what anyone can see: " Science " properly so called, deals not nearly so much with the outward, visible substances of things, as with their qualities and relations, and the forces at work in them. But what are qualities, relations, forces? All, unseen things. You cannot see a quality; you cannot see a force! You blow out a candle in a room, in a moment the smell of that — you know how it is in every corner of the room — yes, that is mere sensation — the element of science comes in, in your working your way from the bare fact of it to the reason of it — to the existence of some force of expansion in the gases thrown out by the smouldering wick, which at once disperses those particles of gas all through the surrounding space. But what

is that force? What really is any force? Nobody knows. The moment you begin to talk
about forces you are among entirely invisible
things and yet they are so real that not only is
science sure of them, but the greater part of
science is concerned with forces; and the great
teachers of science have even worked it out that
different forces can be changed into one another,
so that light can be changed into heat and heat
into gravitation and so forth — and the one
thing they are most sure of is, that no tiniest
quantity of force can be really lost.

You see, you are not in religion here — you
are right on the solid earth — among the most
elementary facts of science, down in the realm of
the commonest substances and products of the
outward nature — and yet — already you cannot move a step without coming right upon
this deep fact in things — that all that you can
see is temporal, passing and changing all the
time — that it is what is unseen in them and
often what is unsee-able that is lasting, permanent.

Look a step higher, into this being and nature
of man, and we are in the midst of the same
truth, coming out in all sorts of ways. There is
the same changing of everything visible in us
— and yet in that is something invisible, which

curiously remains. You know how the visible body is changing all the time. I meet a friend whom I have not seen for twenty years. We say — quite confidently — how glad we are to see each other again. But really, we do not see each other again. Of that which we see, there is no particle that we ever saw before! And yet something has remained the same, all through those 20 years. What is it that has lasted — this " I, myself," this " you " who talk with me about the people and the places we used to be interested in in that former time? What is it that has lasted? Not the seen. Of that which we could see, or which anyone could see then, nothing remains — but something unseen has remained. Do some hesitate to call it soul? Call it mind, call it " x " if you will, the Algebraic sign for something unknown. A little girl, asked what her soul was, answered that it was " her think " — but whatever you call that which has remained in my friend and me, our " mind " our " soul " our " think," it is something invisible. Really, when you come to find how rapidly the changing of all the visible, material part of man is going on, the case is stronger. Why, one who knows about such things, told me the other day that instead of the human body changing once in seven years as we used to be taught at school, it is now known that it hardly lasts a year — much of it is changing, he said, every few weeks; flesh and muscle are dispersed and replaced every four months or so, and I remember being especially struck by his saying that as for the heart, so tremendous is the wear and tear of its constant action that probably every particle of its substance is worn away and replaced in 60 days. But meanwhile there is something in this constantly changing body which does not change — something which moves along through the years, something which keeps the body united and active, gathering from the surrounding universe just the due particles and welding them in, something which is in these things, and yet is more than any or all of them, and keeps this curious personal identity of you and me while all that is visible of you and me is swiftly and constantly changing. The scientist does not know what this " something " is — he tells you frankly that he does not begin to know. It is something his microscope cannot see, his chemical tests cannot find any trace of. They have ransacked the body through and through and they cannot discover it — and yet that invisible element in us is the lasting thing.

You may follow out the same thought as it

touches not the substance of us but our actions, and still it is always true that the seen things are passing, transient, the unseen things the most lasting and real. Can you remember that bad cut, or that wound you had when a youth? Terribly painful, was it not? yes, but it does not hurt you now.   Perhaps there is a scar of it, but it is not painful. But see — was there some great sin that you committed when a youth? That made no mark — not as much visible mark as the cut of a finger, even; — but was it, then, nothing? Why, you feel the pain, the pang of it to-day! Years have passed — you have re-pented that sin — perhaps you have put it ut-terly away, and you feel that God has forgiven you — but still it haunts you at times with a haunting pain, which is entirely unseen, which has nothing visible about it — and yet, how it lasts! — Yes, it is the unseen things that are most permanent!

And even in that larger human action which we call History, we may find illustrations of the same truth. It is not the great visible institu-tions of the world that are most permanent. Think of that great Roman Empire, in one obscure little corner of which Christianity was born! A vast, orderly Empire — with its law courts and its wide, intricate commerce — its

war office, its navy department, its ordered
government reaching from Persia to Britain,
from the forests of Germany to the deserts of
Africa — such an intricate net-work of solid,
responsible rule, that not a village official in
the furthest corner of the empire can scourge
a Roman citizen, however poor, without trem-
bling in his shoes for fear it should be re-
ported! — And there, in one of those furthest
corners, in obscure Nazareth, and Capernaum
— there is a little religious movement among a
few unknown men, a wandering preacher followed by little crowds of country people for a
year or so, and then put to death; a company
of earnest believers clinging to his memory —
drawing together in his name and trying to persuade other men to join them. The whole thing
so invisible, on the visible scale of history, that
the great world knew nothing of it for near a
hundred years; hardly one word about it even
then in the public history of the time. " But the
things which are seen are temporary; the things
which are not seen are permanent." That
mighty world-organism of the Roman Empire
passed away — is now a mere curious study of
the past. That silent invisible force which we
call " faith " and " love " and " hope " which
wrought there in Jesus and his handful of fol-

lowers — that unseen thing lasted, lasts yet, is living still to-day — is working in a million hearts and lives. It is not working as one longs for it to do, and yet I think it is about the most potent force of good in human life! It has kept pleading through the ages and is pleading still, for justice and mercy and all kind and loving charity; it has kept before men a higher ideal of all pure and upright life, given a new remorse for sin, a higher reverence for human life; and here to-day it is making you and me, and millions more, a little more earnest in seeing the right and doing it, and sending thousands and tens of thousands out among the sinful and the suffering on errands of helping and healing and trying to make the world a little happier and better.

And so, wherever we can follow the changes in matter or in man, from the elements which combine to make a leaf or the forces which vibrate through the vast of nature to the something of a subtler personal life which lasts through the changing growth of man and even throbs through history — you have constant illustrations of this great saying of Paul's; that the things which are seen are temporary, but the things which are not seen are permanent.

I do not mean, of course, that Paul worked

all this out, and thought of it, just as his words have set me thinking of it. Paul came upon that thought right up in the highest reaches of it, at once, leaping as it were by one great bound of inspired insight, from the perishing man which was all that could be seen, to the latent invisible child of God, which he could not help believing was in everyone; and from the visible earthly state, to an infinite life " which eye hath not seen nor ear heard." But do not let his high thought be depreciated because he came upon it so, in the heights! That is how men always come upon the highest thoughts, even in science and philosophy and morals and everything! To Copernicus, watching down among the visible movements of earth and stars, which a hundred eyes were following, suddenly there comes a new thought of them — a great unifying thought, which after long trying to make sure of, he tells to the wondering and at first incredulous world. Somewhat so, **to** Paul, plodding on in those old Roman streets, or sitting in the sailmaker's workshop, or the Philippi jail — and taking refuge from his weariness or the pain of his sore scourging in thoughts of Christ and the great blessed Heaven where he would like to be with him — suddenly there would come upon him the sense of how all this

visible world was but a passing vision compared
with the rich and grand realities of God — and
in such an hour — and one fancies, out of many
such hours — flashed up this thought and this
great expression of it, that " we look not at the
things which are seen, but at the things which
are not seen: for the things which are seen are
temporal; but the things which are not seen are
eternal! "

Of course I am not giving what I have said as
any proof! Nature supplies no proof of that absolute categorical kind in anything of man's
higher life. At the most, what Nature gives
are suggestions, confirmations of any great
thought such as this. Paul never proved it;
but he believed it, was certain that it was so,
lived by it, inspired others to live by it; and the
fruit of it, in stronger, nobler, living in the
ages since, has been so sound as to suggest that
it must be really rooted in the realities of the
great world-order. And now we try to look at
its roots — and is it no help to us, is it no confirmation of our thought, to find that even down
among the basal facts of plant and animal and
of man's mere earthly life the very same thing
is constantly true, as far as we can trace? Always something within the seen, deeper than the
seen, something that we cannot see in itself —

but yet we can see that that invisible something
is what lasts and is most permanent! The very
elements that constitute a leaf; the gases into
which a lump of coal may be dispersed; — the
something — mind, soul, life, or what you will,
which lives on through a score of changes in
everything that makes up the human body —
No! these do not prove that unseen something is
to live on, even past the body's final collapse.
No! But such things everywhere in Nature
send me back to the teachings of Paul and of
Paul's greater Lord, with a renewed confidence
— confidence that their grand words of an un-
dying life were not the inflated guesses of conceit but the inspired insight of the pure in heart.
And there I rest — there where so many hearts
have rested through the ages, I would have us
all to rest. By all means let us investigate
everything to the furthest that we can. Look
into all this wonderful science which is the
glory of our time; only take in as really part
of it not just the heiroglyphics of stone and
plant and star, but the far clearer writing in the
conscious life of man. Yes, certainly God made
the stone and plant and star, and what they tell
me is surely His Word, but just as surely he
made man, and his meeting is plainer in the
great trend of human thought; and in God's

holiest, the word comes out not in such broken syllables as I can spell from rock or plant but in great golden sentences of light that make a glory wherever they shine into man's heart and life.   So let us have faith; Life is not a delusion even at its lowest — let us not fear that it can play us false at its highest.   As Emerson said —

"   All things excellent,
As God lives, are permanent."

The " life to come is just as real as this — yes, it is this — this — lasting not only beyond the body of to-day, or of next year, but beyond all visible things, among the unseen things which are eternal!

ON BELIEF IN THINGS WHICH CANNOT BE PROVED

IN THE old time, men asked for " signs." In these days what they ask, is, *proof*. I do not think it is an " evil generation," and its doubt, especially, is honest and earnest doubt. But certainly it is a generation that seeks, after its better fashion, for a " sign." Men come to Christianity as once those Jews came to Christ. " We want all this unmistakably proved," they say. " These thoughts and feelings which claim such authority over life, — belief in God and immortality, even conscience and the moral law, — what are these things? We want some sign, some proof of them which there can be no possible gainsaying." And when they find that no such proof can be given, many would put these things aside, as altogther unreal.

So I take for my subject — " Belief in things which cannot be proved." Perhaps at first sight the very statement of the subject seems to discredit it. The bare idea seems contrary to the

scientific spirit of the age. Men have become so
accustomed to the precise statements and verifications of science; to having everything set down
in black and white, to the thousandth of an inch
or a fourth decimal, that they cannot endure to
have anything left vague or uncertain. And
yet I am bold enough to say that all this idea
of having everything "proved," logical and
plausible, as it may seem, is really curiously delusive; that life does not go by "proofs"; that
thought, judgment, feeling, action, are seldom
based on "proofs." And so, though the highest things in life may not prove themselves,
cannot be proved, that is no reason for doubting
their reality, yes and that they may be the very
grandest realities.

Let us begin at "the small end" of this subject. It is curious to see, how this questioning
age, which would insist so strongly on logical
proof in the great things of the inner life, really
answers itself in the small things of the outer
life. Why, the world could not go on for a day
if it would not believe anything, nor act on its
belief, till it could be proved. The real conduct
of life proceeds on impressions accepted directly
from the senses, or on habits of thought re-
ceived from the past, or on convictions gradually
consolidated by experience. Hardly ever, is any

single thing, if you bring it rigidly to book, capable of absolute proof. It is only an impression that I exist — though a strong one. My impression that you exist, as thinking personal beings, is even less capable of proof; it is a mere inference from certain sensations on my optic nerve. Yet I know that such sensations may be entirely delusive, for I felt them just as unmistakably about the people I saw in my dreams last night. Does man wait to eat and drink till it shall be proved to him that food is necessary? By all means demonstrate to me the principles of digestion, — but I would like my breakfast first, the demonstration afterwards. Will you wait to go down to the city on business till you have faced and settled the question whether there is any real, external world, and logically proved that even the omnibus is anything but a subjective idea? To any philosophical idealist who wanted you to assure yourself on this matter, you would say — "we had better get into this thing, which appears like a real omnibus, and we can argue whether there really is such a thing as we go along." I am not jesting. Every close thinker knows that, in reality, all the most fundamental elements of our living have to be taken for granted, are, really, only more or less vivid impressions, absolutely incapable of rigid

demonstration. And so of all the realm of feel
ing and emotion :—

> "I do not love thee, Doctor Fell
> The reason, why, I cannot tell."

Do our likes and dislikes go by proving? Nay,
we not only constantly believe, and feel, and
act, without proof, but one of the most common
things in life is an actual distrust of the offer
of proof. Those columns after columns in the
papers, of "proofs" of some infallible remedy,
— well, those testimonials of cure seem overwhelming, but you are incredulous all the same.
So, if some public official is always challenging
investigation, you get an impression that in reality there is something *not* quite right. And I
think we carry the same feeling into deeper
things. I know that some very good people believe in spiritualism, and of course it is simply
a question of whether or not it is true. But I
own I should be inclined to think more of the
probabilty of its being true if it were not so
very largely occupied in proving itself, always
asking to be "tested," and obligingly ready to
give any quantity of "signs." When something
comes that claims to be a communication out
of the Divine heights — let me simply hear the
word — if it is from the Divine, it will surely bear

some marks of it in itself. A great truth carries its own conviction with it.

Now you see the significance of the Jews coming to Christ, and asking for a sign — not these little healing words for poor sick folk — there is an emphasis on that "sign from Heaven" — something that there could be no doubt about — and you see, too, why Christ so utterly refused anything of the kind. Let it be an open question, what that strange power was that Christ had over the sick body or the disordered mind; it was at any rate something that he shrank from making a show of, or using as a mere weapon against unbelief. " He that hath ears to hear, let him hear!" That was his appeal. He stood among his people — just one of themselves, not with any "sign," not even in any prophet's garb, — the simple Man of Nazareth — but with a gospel which made its own way, and at length laid hold of the heart of the world, simply because it did come to men as a revealing of Divine things, and made Duty, and God, and Heaven, more real to the human soul than they had ever been before. But that gospel had to make its way, by this intense impression it made, not by its being *proved*. And it has always been so, and is so still. One is sometimes challenged to "prove" Christianity.

They might as well challenge one to prove
Shakespeare's plays or Mendelsohn's music.
These things are not matters of proof. So with
Christianity. Here is this "Gospel according
to Luke" as it is named, with these parables
of "the good Samaritan" and "the Prodigal
Son" Can it be absolutely proved, that Luke
wrote this gospel, and that Jesus actually spoke
those parables just so? No! It cannot be
categorically proved. I have little doubt that it
was so. I think it is as fairly established that
those are Christ's teaching, as any ancient
authorship can be expected to be. But the real
power of those parables does not rest on their
being proved, but upon the impression they
make. Light is light, and it helps you to see,
even if you cannot quite make out where it
comes from. And these great parables have
somehow made our relation to man and to God
a little clearer. And so with Christ's life and
teachings as a whole. The great fact is, that
these have stirred and helped the world as nothing else has ever done. Proofs of a kind, they
have given in plenty: — the proofs of lives made
better, of noble movements for human good, of
human society helped, though slowly, to higher
thoughts and ways. Real proofs these, in the
deepest fact of things. The truth about num-

bers, must be proved by figures. The truth about substances, must be proved by weight or measure or chemical test. The truth about life is proved by living. But any exact, logical demonstration? — No! None such was forthcoming for Christ's own time, and none can be made out now. Yet he took hold upon the heart of the world, and he keeps it. There are more people in the world to-day, reverencing his name, studying his life, trying to be truer, kinder men and women for his sake, then ever before. As the corruptions of the dark ages are gradually clearing away, and the simple Gospel figure stands out in its original tenderness and power, Christ remains more manifestly than ever the grandest leader of our race, the divinest spiritual influence in history.

Thinking of all this, seeing how it has been with Christ and his great words, I feel my trust strengthened, not in these alone, but in all the moral and religious side of life, not just in their Christian aspect, but as integral parts of the being and growth of man.

Take the moral life. What is that voice of conscience? What is it — that which speaks in the heart of the grown man or the little child, of this being right, and that, wrong? Why should you attend to that restraining influence?

You know, if you shall challenge that subtle feeling for a logical proof of itself, it can never give one. You may easily argue conscience down, not so as to silence it, indeed, but so as to persuade yourself that it is nothing but a fancy, that the distinction between right and wrong is a mere scruple of man's own inventing. And it does not strive nor cry. There is no compulsion to righteousness. Often, men wish there were. Perhaps this is one of the most touching forms of this craving for " signs " and certainty, — a man being drawn down by sin, and struggling against it — but feeling so pitifully weak. " Oh, that God would rend the heavens and come down," and by some palpable manifestation overawe the tempted heart and make it impossible to sin. But no; no sign is given, and when the sin is sinned, still no sign. The sun shines on; birds sing; the flowers do not turn away their heads; men come and go; the world goes on unchanged. Yet is the difference between right and wrong, therefore, nothing? Why, there is no distinction of form or colour, sweetness or sourness, or anything in the outward world, to compare with it for a moment. It is quite impalpable. It gives no outward sign. No closest test can analyse it. It cannot be proved to be anything, — and yet

— the difference between right and wrong is the most awful and tremendous thing in all man's being, and in all the Universe.

Or — take Religion. What are these shadowy impulses which through the ages point man's heart towards God, and towards the sense of some further life? "Man," said Dr. Martineau, "does not believe in immortality because it has ever been proved; but he is for ever trying to prove it, because he cannot help believing it." So with belief in God. Oh, how mankind has longed for some unmistakable manifestation of Deity. It is no craving of *our* age alone. The old world idolatries came of it. It was so hard to realise the invisible. Men wanted some visible embodiment of this Divine presence which seemed to haunt them. Here and there some strong souled Moses might be able to do without anything visible, and might thunder against all graven images, but the common people still cried to the weaker Aaron, "make us Gods!" To-day the craving takes a different form. It does not ask an outward presentation of God, so much as a logical proof of Him. It wants that mysterious Life demonstrating to science. It wants reason to prove the existence of God. Then, some say, — "it is by intuition that the soul discerns Him"; — and how many strain

that gaze of their souls, that intense scrutiny
of the thoughts and impressions that come to
them in the awe of Night or in the stillness of
prayer — trying to make out something which
they can distinctly recognise as God. And here,
too, they get discouraged — often it seems as
if the more eagerly they strain their mental
gaze, the more they cannot see that Higher presence. I believe that this is one of the commonest
phases of that doubt which is so frequent to-
day, and which is so anxious for some scientific
proof. Some of you may remember how Pro-
fessor Tyndall proposed to organise a prayer-
test — two Hospitals to be set apart, and the
patients treated with equal skill, only the one set
to be prayed for, and the other not, and the result to decide whether prayer amounts to anything. When that was proposed, religious men
at once universally refused to submit *Prayer* to
any such material test, — and I remember that
their refusal was sneered at by some as showing
that they had no real faith in God. But that
laughter was shallow. These deep things of
man's inner life, are, simply, not subjects for
such outward tests, however much they may
really affect the outward life. I believe for instance that righteousness affects the outward
life; that honesty is " the best policy " even for

mere wordly success. Yet suppose some one, who has set up the theory that there is no real difference between right and wrong, to challenge me to stake my moral faith upon the comparative fortunes of twenty honest men, and twenty clever rogues, — shall I agree to do so? Not for a moment! Not by such outward proofs and signs can these deep things of the conscience and the inner life be demonstrated. Take this very *life* itself in us, apart from this or that special quality or phase of it. As I look into your face, just with my ordinary eyesight as we stand talking together, I perceive in you a life, of thought, intelligence, feeling — answering to this life I am conscious of in myself. But suppose for some reason, I begin to distrust my eyesight. I say — "Let us look into this appearance of life more closely; let us see exactly what it is." And I bring my microscope, and apply it to your face. Shall I see the life in you more clearly? The very opposite. The more powerful my microscope, the more it will magnify the mere fleshly tissue, but the more absolutely I shall lose the expression of personal life. So, in scores of ways, the very effort after exact proof, really makes the deepest things less evident, not more so, — even when they are unmistakably real. Sometimes a larger, general

view shows things of which the close scrutiny
shows nothing. Can you see that the atmosphere
has any colour as you look at the few yards of
air before you? No! But look up through the
fifty miles of air into the solemn depths of the
sky, and you see that beautiful blue as plainly
as if it was painted on the next wall. So as
you look at the religious sense in your own individual thought and feeling, all may seem unsubstantial, nothing clear enough to take as any
real discerning of God. But don't look at your
own thought and feeling; look at the thought
and feeling of humanity; look along the cen
turies; see how religion has come out in the
larger life of mankind! See how, in such different forms, it has yet in some form risen in
every race, and intertwined itself (like the basal
instincts of hunger, love, or gain) through all
of human doings. See what a tremendous force
it has been, even when wrested to the side of
evil; but how much more it has inspired man's
noblest works, lifted man to the loftiest heroism.
Talk of giving it up because it cannot be logically proved to us to-day? Why, nothing can be
absolutely proved, — and yet things are; and
greatest of all the things that *are* are the invisible things; and greatest of the invisible
things are these of conscience and soul and God.

They are only in the same category, really, with everything else. As the life of man rises in the scale, it rises more and more above the mere *outward,* into a higher range of thought, perception, motive. This is so not in science only; — art, music, the great thoughts of thinkers, the lofty ideals of goodness, the uplifting aspirations of worship — all of these are things which hide their secret from all outward sense, and yet they are life's noblest elements, life without them is a bare, poor, hopeless thing!

The practical help of all this, is here: — to teach us to look out a little more humbly and reverently in this wondrous universe and wondrous life in which we find ourselves. We want a little less of that common assumption of knowl edge, or of expecting to know, and that we have only to concern ourselves with what we know; and at the same time, we do not want to fall into the other extreme of a hopeless agnosticism, but to keep on our way in confident and happy faith. What? Be discouraged because we cannot *know* or prove life's highest things? Why, what we know or even think we know, is only the very smallest, most superficial part of everything. Your most defined knowledge opens out, right upon an unsearchable infinity. You can measure a foot, a mile, — but what is

this thing space? You can measure an hour, a
year, — but what is time — still more, what is
eternity? What then? Would you stop at the
measurements or time-beats that you think you
know, and lose the uplifting wonder of that
larger infinity to which they directly lead? For
so do all things lead us. The " flower in the
crannied wall " leads you right to the whole
mystery of the universe. A little child's face,
the more you look into it shadows forth possibilities that reach to Heaven. A parent's love,
as you ponder its deepest meaning, opens to you
the sense of some source of love in this great
universe, in which there is no stopping place
short of faith in God. All things are hints to
us, — not proofs, but hints, leadings, towards
greater things of which we catch glimpses, and
which as the ages pass make themselves felt.
And these greater things, like the great Christ,
while giving no signs or proofs, invite our hearts
to believe in them and follow them. Man's
wisdom is, while holding fast the clue of what
he sees and knows — hold that fast, there is
the safeguard against folly and superstition —
but, holding fast that clue of what he sees and
knows let him go on with glad, upward-looking
faith into the realm beyond. Let life lie open
to the greater things, and be growing towards

them; keep a welcoming eye for the world's tender, solemn beauty; obey the promptings of the best and kindest thoughts that lead you on to things you have not done, perhaps are afraid to do; keep touch with the great adoring habit of the world; dare to lift up your song and prayer with the earth's manifold worship, albeit when you try to make out some clear outline of that you worship, your thought falls back dazed and blinded. And then, although these greater realities may never prove themselves in figures or in syllogisms, they shall gradually prove themselves in life. Still to the end, we may not see, but we shall be more and more sure that we are in the way towards seeing, — tending not towards nothingness and darkness, but towards the absolute reality and towards the perfect light.

THE MYSTERY OF MIND

PAUL here touches one of the deep perplexities of life. I have called it the perplexity of mind. In the deepest aspect of it, I might as well couple the perplexity of matter with that of mind, for really matter, what matter is, is just as obscure, just as much a mystery as what mind is. But we do not feel it so. To the ordinary apprehension, at least, there does not seem any particular perplexity about outward material things. A tree, a rock, a horse, no mistake about these; no doubt as to their being facts and realities. But if I speak of mind, or of conscience or soul or any of what we commonly call mental or spiritual realities, there are many who at once find doubts and questionings suggested. How do we know that there is any such thing as soul or mind? If there is, why is it not just as palpable to us as the body is? That is the perplexity. Because, this subtler side of life and being haunts man. We cannot live together a day or an hour without talking of mind or conscience or some other element of that invisible side of our nature. We talk of "making up our mind" or "changing our mind" or "obeying conscience" or "keeping a pure soul." And it seems as if, supposing these are realities, there ought to be no more doubt about them, we ought to be able to lay our hands upon them, and say, "See, here it is, just thus and so." But you know it is just the opposite. If it were not, I should not have to be working out an argument of this kind. I do not have to argue to help people to realise that trees and rocks and bodies are real. But we do constantly need to reassure ourselves that mind and soul and conscience are real, yes and indeed the most tremendous realities of all.

Now let us look at the two sides of this perplexity a little more fully. On the one hand is the material universe — a glorious thing to contemplate, even to any one who merely looks at it from the outside as it were, with what Paul calls "the natural eye." To the trained eye and to the assisted eye, it grows more and more wonderful. Year by year the microscope in one direction and the telescope in the other are opening the Universe to our gaze in ever more wonderful gloriousness and extent. Chemistry seems the great science to-day, penetrating to the very innermost secrets of all this physical being. But the point is, the orderly observableness of it all. Not an object, not a force, not a fact, not the tiniest spot of space, but science claims it for its own, and never leaves it till it has reduced it to its own terms, in the catalogue of material things, and classed it upon the shelves of system and law. And even far beyond any direct observation, it makes the finer forces, it discovers work for it, and keeps tracking things out and making them visible to thought if not to sight. The photographic plate indicates stars that are far beyond the power of any telessope to shew us. The Röntgen rays, the finer workings of electricity, are quite invisible; but by curious cross-tracks of subtle analysis they are being brought within the range of knowledge. And as with the material universe so with these bodies of ours; the body has been looked through and through. Every atom takes its place in the material order. The brain has been weighed and analysed, and its various nervous tissues tracked to their local uses; and science has got behind the delicate mechanism of the eye; and watches the formation of the tiny cells by which new matter replaces life's decay and waste; and the very blood has been analysed and watched to find what its red or white corpuscles have to do in the harming or helping of life.

There is the physical Universe, and man's
body in its place in it. Yet, are these all? Not
at all! Somehow, the very capacity of all this
to be observed and every use noted; the very
orderly completeness of this whole outward Universe only brings out in stronger relief the fact
of their being quite a whole range of being
which at the same time is existing or going on:
— the whole range of human living and thinking — of what we call intellectual, moral and
spiritual living and acting! Leave out the question of whether we may speak of mind and soul.
But we cannot help speaking of thinking and
feeling. And thought, say, lies just as utterly
outside the scope of the material world as the
" mind " or " spirit " we are enquiring about.
Just look for a moment at this intangible range
of facts and see what an immense part it plays
in life. Think of love and hatred, two of the
most tremendous powers by which the human
world is moved. Think of the sense of shame,
the dreadful consciousness of guilt; — and on
the other hand the joy of being able to do a
kind, helpful action. Think of that feeling of
exerting one's will. And all these are only in-
cidental developments of a still more wonderful
consciousness — that of personal existence, that
which is able to say " I — myself." Now here

is the greater part of life! What of it? Are we to ignore it — nay, we cannot do that if we would — but are we to doubt about it and discredit it, because our science, which in the great outward Universe seems so minute and exhaustive, can simply tell us nothing about it? It is curious how absolutely it does lie outside the cognizance of our science. I cut or burn my finger — there is the physical fact plain on the surface of things; science can tell me all about it. Suppose I violate my conscience, do something that I feel to be sinful — why, there is no physical change whatever, and yet somewhere, somehow, we feel that the sense of wrong-doing is one of the most tremendous facts of our being, — one, in the presence of which mere cuts or burns sink into insignificance. I move my arm: — that too is a demonstrable fact, science can watch it, measure it, tell all about it. I make what I call a movement of thought — I calculate a sum, or I think out those words I am now saying to you. Does any one doubt that this last kind of movement is a far greater fact in my being than any mere muscular movement? Here, you see, is a whole side of our living — thought, anger, love, conscientiousness, will — just as much facts as seeing, hearing, digestion, or the circulation of the blood — and our science is simply helpless among them, cannot even discern or distinguish them, any more than the ear can distinguish colours; and are we then to treat this range of imperceptible feelings, including all that is commonly classed under conscience and soul, as something vague and doubtful, or as lying so far in among the microscopic recesses of being, that the reliable nature of them has not yet been discovered. But they do not lie far in or deep down. If you see a man strike a little child, your moral sense of horror is just as quick, just as palpable as your sight of the mere muscular movement. Will you trust the eye, because it is an evident thing, and man has found out its nature and how it works; and then will you distrust the moral sense, because science cannot tell you what it is or anything about it? And even where the material sight gives you the strongest impression of this unknown element of mind and personal character being somehow closely connected with the body, it does not do so in a way which suggests some infinitesimally finer element in the recesses of our being, which scientific investigation has not yet got to — the impression lies on the very surface. I see the indication of it in a man's face. What is it? It is not colour, it is not form. Science can note these for me; but it cannot touch that matter of the expression which evidences the life. And if it cannot touch it at the surface, it certainly cannot by going deeper in or making its examination minuter. If the general perception of the eye is too vague for me to dare to infer *mind* from my friend's face, certainly it will not become more perceptible through a microscope! On the contrary, if you examine the face with a microscope to try to get closer into the indication of the mind, the more powerful the lense, only the more utterly will it lose all trace of mind and come back to mere common matter, only magnified. What does all this lead to? That if only we keep on making our tests more minute we shall at last capture these curious elements of thought and consciousness? No! I think science is rather coming to the conclusion that it is not getting nearer to the mystery of mind that way. It rather seems as if we have to frankly recognise that there is some other different element in the make up of a man — different from anything we know as bodily or material — something which, even if (as the Monist philosophy maintains) it is ultimately of the same nature as matter, is in so infinitely finer a form, that it cannot be judged by any limitations of what we know as matter. Even if we had to conclude that what we call the higher life in man, cannot be known at all, directly, still it is the higher life; and if we only know it by its results, still these are of a kind which lift it clear above that lower bodily life of which we seem to have some knowledge. So, no possible inference as to the source of things could make friendship a dream, or conscience a delusion, or lessen the force of that conviction which has grown up among these higher elements that somehow they live on even when the lower elements dissolve.

But I want to give you something better than my own thoughts. Years ago, when I was feeling this mystery of mind an actual perplexity, something that a little weakened my hold on moral and spiritual things, and when I was glad of any light, one of the things that really helped me was a little poem of Francis Turner Palgrave's. I came upon it again quite lately, and read it again with some interest to see if it would seem still to have the same helpful force of thought in it. And it seemed still so strong that I thought I would like to quote some parts of it. It is called the "Reign of Law" and its key-note is whence and whither. And it is a plea, in the fuller light of Law itself, for faith in the soul and its immortality. The poem imagines some mourners by the dead Christ; loving watchers and mourners by that noblest of the dead, but possessed by that overwhelming sense of Law, and unable to believe in anything even in their Christ, except matter, perishing matter:

> " We ne'er have seen the law
>   Reversed, 'neath which we lie;
> Exceptions none are found,
>   And when we die, we die!"

— And I take up the poem just as it breaks in upon them with this apostrophe:

> " Then, wherefore are ye come?
>   Why watch a worn out corse?
> Why weep a ripple, past
>   Down the long stream of force?
>
> The forces that were Christ,
>   Have ta'en new forms, and fled
> The common sun goes up,
>   The dead are with the dead.
>
> 'Twas but a phantom life,
>   That seemed to think and will
> Evolving Self and God
>   By some suggestive skill
> That had its day of passage hither,
> But knew no whence, and knows no whither.

If this be all in all,
  Life but one mode of force,
Law but the plan which binds
  The sequences in course:
All essence, all design,
  Shut out from mortal ken,
We bow to Nature's fate,
  And drop the style of men;
The summer dust the wind wafts hither
Is not more dead to whence and whither.

But if our life be life,
  And thought and will and love,
Not vague unconscious airs
  That o'er wild harp strings move;
If consciousness be aught
  Of all it seems to be
And souls are something more
  Than lights that gleam and flee—
Though dark the road that leads us hither,
The heart must ask its whence and whither.

To matter or to force,
  The all is not confined,
Beside the law of things
  Is set the law of mind.
One speaks in rock and star
  And one within the brain
In unison at times,
  And then apart again.

The sequences of Law,
  We learn through mind alone,

'Tis only through the soul
  That aught we know, is known.
With equal voice she tells
  Of what we touch and see
Within these bounds of life,
  And of a life to be.
Proclaiming One who brought us hither
And holds the keys of whence and whither.

And then he breaks into such an exultation in
this sense of the reality of soul in man! —

"Oh, shrine of God, that now
  Must learn itself with awe!
O, heart and soul that move
  Beneath a living law!
That which seemed all the rule,
  Of Nature, is but part;
A larger, deeper law,
  Claims also soul and heart.

We may not hope to read
  Or understand the whole,
Or of the law of things,
  Or of the law of soul.
E'en in the eternal stars
  Dim perturbations rise,
And all the searcher's search
  Does not exhaust the skies;
He who has framed and brought us hither
Holds in his hands the whence and whither.

He in his science plans,
  What no known laws foretell;

The wandering fires and fixed,
　Alike are miracle!
The common death of all,
　The life renewed above,
Are both within the scheme
　Of that all-circling love!
The seeming chance that cast us hither,
Accomplishes His Whence and Whither!

Of course it may be said that this is still only affirmation, and that affirmation does not become proof merely by being clothed in poetry. No! but then it is not a question of proof — for, as Tennyson says —

"Nothing worthy proving can be proved,
　Nor yet disproven....."

All that higher side of life which we indicate — not define — by the words "mental" or "spiritual" depends really upon its own affirmation within us; and whatever brings out the sense of it more vividly helps us to feel a quiet certainty that though we cannot tell just what or how it is, it is the noblest and the most reliable element in us.

And so from these perplexities about mind and soul, which the exactness and certainty of physical science has started up with new force in our day, we have simply to fall back upon our inner consciousness, backed as it is by the common consciousness of man, and the clear sense of the wisest and the holiest. Occasionally this higher consciousness seems confused or obscured, as many subtle thinkers have found it in our time; but the quiet heart of man and the silent teaching of experience keeps leading back to the recognition of mind, conscience, soul, as, however mysterious, still the greatest realities of Being.

And when we come to this (to live in it and rest in it, Mind, Conscience, Soul, life's greatest realities) it leads us further still, still not in outlined knowledge, but in very strong and happy faith — faith reaching outside our life, above, beyond — that this conscious life in us is not the only conscious life in a vast machinery of substances and forces! It is life in an answering Universe of life, Soul in an answering universe of Spirit, Conscience in an answering Universe of Righteous Will; and human friendliness and love in an answering Universe that has a kindred, mighty Loving-Kindness in its inmost and divinest heart and meaning.

THE VERIFICATION OF MIND

I HAVE been considering the mystery of mind. Why are not conscience and soul, and all that we are conscious of in that vague region which we call mind, why are not these as palpable as the body? And I urged strongly that even if all that, which we speak of as the " higher life " in man, cannot be known directly, still it evidently is the higher life, and we may trust it, backed, as it is by the common consciousness of man and the clear sense of the wisest and holiest.

But I think that we may go a little further, and it is that further step that I would now trace.

Even if we could be no surer of any of these invisible things — than simply to say, ' well, we feel so and so '; even if we were left to this general thought and feeling of them as things in our minds — even so we should not be badly off. Because, we feel them quite unmistakably, even though we cannot tell how. My feelings on hearing of a brutal murder are just as clear and unmistakable as my outward sensation of this desk, or of this light. But that mere feeling, strong, intense as it is, is not all. When **we** look into it, we find that the intimations of our inner consciousness are just as capable of being verified as those of the outward senses. Nay, more, — the very methods of verification are curiously alike.

Let us range clearly, side by side, these two distinct classes of impressions which make themselves felt in our nature — on the one hand those coming from the outside, in such sensations as sight, touch, sound, reporting to us the nature and relations of material objects; on the other hand, the impressions rising up within us, as it were, and making us aware of invisible qualities and existences. As a fact men have taken both sets of impressions as trustworthy. Trusting the outward sensations, they have built up their science of the laws and relations of out ward things. Taking the inner consciousness as trustworthy, they have built up its perceptions of mind, and soul, into mental science, Morals, Law, Religion. The question is, of course, how we can be sure that either set of impressions corresponds to anything that really is? Even the vividneess of the outward sensation as your eye sees a thing and your hand touches it, is no sure proof. We know that some such sensations are delusions. When you are dreaming, you have for the time just as vivid an impression of the things and people in that dream-state, as, now in your waking hours, you have of the person sitting next to you. Yet you know that those dream impressions have no reality. How? How do you verify that some are realities, while others are only dreams?

Well, there are several well-understood qualities which we find in the impressions of our waking-hours, but not in our dreams, and which verify for us some permanent reality in those things of our waking-hours. And what I am struck with, is, that, really, there are the same verifications in mental and moral and spiritual things, to make us sure that these, too, are not mere fancies, but subtle realities, — parts, though all invisible of the ordered reality of things. One of these tests of the external realities, is, that they are seen and felt by others, very much as by ourselves. This at once cuts them off from mere dreams or fancies. You and I might be asleep and dreaming in the same room, but the things and people we should see in our dreams would be perfectly different. The moment we wake, we see the same things. Is there a book before us, it is a book to both. A lamp? Each sees it as a lamp. But now see! The reality of that invisible world of

thought and mind, is confirmed in the same way.
Men are just as universally conscious of the
things of thought and mind, as they are of outward visible things, go where you will among
men, you find the same feelings of love and
hate, of right and wrong, of will, of personality;
and of these things in each other as well as in
oneself. As these things are perceived within,
it may not be so easy to compare exact notes
about them. You cannot place a thought or a
feeling on the table before you like a botanical
specimen. But we can compare notes quite sufficiently to be sure there is no mistake. The
quality of deceitfulness is the same thing to one
man's inner perception that it is to another's.
If a dozen of us see a man striking a little child,
we see the invisible quality of the act, just as
clearly and as much alike, as we see the outward
movement. And so even of religious realities.
Just as, mankind through, you find this moral
sense, of distinction between right and wrong,
so you find a religious sense of some mighty life
in or through nature, with which man's being is
somehow connected; and all this tells us that this
common consciousness of inner invisible things,
is just as trustworthy as the sensations of an
outward visible world.

I may carry the parallel to a second step, to

a further method of verification. There is something about these physical sensations which seem to tell us of an outward world, more striking than their being felt by all people alike, — and that is that they fit together, can be compared and made subjects of calculation and experiment. That is what makes science possible. You could not have a science of the objects which you see in your dream, however vivid and real they may seem at the moment. Edmund Halley, in 1682 saw what, to him, was a new star — a comet. It did not seem more real at the time, than a star I saw in a dream some nights ago. But see: he watches his star's course, calculated that it ought to return in 76 years, that would be in 1758; and others, later, revising his calculations made out that it ought to return about April, 1759, — and lo: in March 1759 it reappeared, in March, within one month of the date; and then they calculated more closely again, and in 1835 it rounded the sun within 3 days of the time they had figured. But nobody can do that with the dream-star!

Well, the same verification holds for all this realm of things we perceive by thought or mind. There is the significance of Paul's word about " comparing spiritual things with spiritual." It is just as easy to compare the impressions which two characters, or two thoughts make upon the inner sense, as to compare the impressions which two bodies or substances make upon the eye. True, the inner impressions have no distinct outline, but they are far more intense. My inner sense of the invisible difference between a good man, and a base scoundrel, is far intenser than any outward sense of the difference in their persons. And it is by trusting this inner sense, about qualities, and ideas, and motives and all sorts of invisible things that all human law has grown up, and all Philosophy and all Religion. What do all the world's vast institutions of Justice rest upon? What is " justice "? A purely invisible quality, and yet all the institutions built upon that invisible quality, are just as stable and certain as the systems of Science built on the visible properties 'of things. And so with Re ligion, in the deepest ultimate fact of it. Religion in the deepest fact of it, seems to be a sort of instinctive sense of life behind the veil of Nature; life, and meaning, in Nature's movements, something as man discerns life and meaning behind the veil of flesh in his fellow man. From comparison of their varying impressions of this life behind Nature men have risen from the first rude fetichism to the highest thoughts of Religion. Even where, in its higher ranges, the sense of Divine communication, has come in, it is still by comparison of impressions which are quite impalpable to any outward sense that the prophet has come to be sure that God is leading him, and that Christ can say: " The words that I speak unto you, I speak not of myself." There, in the highest experience, that inner world of souls, and goodness, and God, becomes actually more real than all the outward world of trees and stones and the moving bodies of men.

There is yet one more verification by which men justify their belief in the reality of the external world, and which is really just as strong for justifying our belief in the world of mind. I mean — the proof by action and life. We verify our sensations of outward things, not only by comparing what we think we see and feel, with what others see and feel; and, not only by finding that the knowledge so obtained by ourselves and others can be combined into system and science, — but, crowning test of all, we verify these sensations, and the science so elaborated from them by acting upon them. If a man should refuse to admit that his bodily sensations — sight, touch, hearing and so forth, are anything, any indications of corresponding realities — simply he would soon cease to live. If he should refuse to accept the science men have elaborated by comparison and calculations based on sight, touch and hearing, he might live indeed, but it would be simply the life of the savage. And the same reasoning will lead on to living with the same trust and sense of reality in all the higher range of the intellectual, moral and spiritual, — all the world of mind. This is an orderly, ordered world all through. Man rises from physical facts to physical laws. But in the very progress which leads him on to laws at all, he comes to qualities of character. " Character," " qualities " — all invisible, but yet very real! And the verification by action and life, if it applies in material things, is worth infinitely more in moral and spiritual things. Talk of the mischief which would come of a man's refusing to believe in his sensations of sight or touch, what is that compared with the mischief which would come of his refusing to believe in his inner consciousness of truth, right, goodness! Practically man cannot ignore that inner, moral and spiritual consciousness. He may refuse to attend to it; he may neglect to observe its finer teaching, but he cannot help feeling something of it. And even in his neglect, he will verify it! If you neglect and disregard moral and spiritual perceptions you bring as great a discord and confusion into life,

as by any ignoring of physical facts or laws —
nay, a greater, more terrible discord. It is even
worse to run your head against a moral law, than
to run it against a physical law. There may be
no outward scar to shew for it; the slightest
bodily bruise makes more visible mark that
science can note, than the breaking of half the
commandments does, but none the less life is
injured in its very innermost and intensest being. It is so, even at the very beginning of
moral and spiritual life; but it is when you look
at life in its higher and nobler developments that
this verification of all the realm of mind is most
striking. When you come face to face with any
man who has really trusted this consciousness of
mind and soul and conscience and affection, and
lived in it, a word of his deep experience shews
that it is realities he has found, and in which he
has lived. And yet here, precisely, it is (in the
case of those who have most believed in moral
and spiritual things, and most acted on their belief) here it is that, if their course has been
based on delusion, it would show most conspicuously. If the astronomer has reckoned a
casual gleam or some flaw in his lense, as one
of the stars by which he is to measure the mighty
distances of space, why, the more accurately he
calculates and works from his false premises, and

the further he works on his calculation, so much the larger and more palpable will be the error and confusion of the result. So if the moral law of conscience be a fancy of ours that we have imported and hypothecated into a Universe that has only material law in it; if soul be a mere conceit of our own self-consciousness, and if God be only a mirage on the horizon of things produced by a want of clearness in our sight, it will be those who have most taken conscience and soul and God into their account, and lived by their belief, whose results in life should exhibit the most palpable blunder and the most chaotic confusion. But I look to those who have most treated soul and conscience and God as realities, and it is with them that confusion disappears. I look into their lives and by those lives I know that their faith is not, at least in its deep basis, a blunder. Of course they may differ, and make mistakes about these things. All attempts to define or describe these impalpable realities of mind, — must be more or less imperfect, but in the deep basis of their faith, it is justified and verified by life.

And now, what does it all come to? This is not a matter of abstract theorizing, still less of intricate word-fencing. I have set all this before you because I believe that it touches the very heart of our daily practical living. The fact is that in the brilliant and wonderful advances of our time in the exploration of the outward Universe and the Physical man, men are getting to feel as if these were all, at least all that is certain and reliable. And they are not all! They are not even half! They are only the coarsest, poorest, grossest part! Infinitely nobler, grander, more deeply and unchangeably real, is that strange element of life which stirs within us, we know not how, and seems almost like another subtler universe! Of the outward material Universe, I suppose we know in our modern science, a hundred times as much as did the ancient world; and it is little wonder perhaps that we fall to thinking that there is nothing like it. Of that inner world of life and mind — we do not know much more than Plato knew when he tried to analyse Mind, or than Christ felt when he said "The life is more than meat." Now, as then, we touch it, here and there, in a few great words, Soul, Affection, Will, Conscience, and, over all, God — words which we still cannot define but which faintly touch and signify for us life's greatest, infinitely greatest realities. We want to have more faith in this intangible and yet so real side of Being. We want to trust in it more, to live in it more, to give it a larger, fuller part in our thinking and working! For this is the eternal element in things! The earth changes; Man's noblest frame decays. All man's earthly treasure fades and dies; but Mind, Soul, Affection, Conscience and the Divine Oversoul, these are for ever and for ever!

THE BUGBEAR OF THE UNKNOWABLE

I THINK it is a help, in the doubts and perplexities of our own time, to see how in far older
and different times, men have felt very much the
same doubt or perplexity as we do. To read
how the Arabian Poet who is supposed to have
written the Book of Job, cries out " Canst thou
by searching find out God?" and how the
greatest of the Hebrew prophets, longing for the
Divine Vision, could only say " Verily thou art
a God that hidest thyself!" while yet they never
lost their faith — makes it is a little easier to us
still to believe and love and pray, even though
the longing search of the human mind is still, in
the last resort, baffled, and even though some
would counsel us to give up the whole subject as
hopelessly belonging to " the unknown." You
often hear it said: " Religion is a subject of
which no one can really know anything!" and
it is said so confidently, and as if it were a self-
evident fact, that it is difficult to resist the impression of it. Now it seems to me that this
reiteration of " the unknown " is being rather

overdone.   It is becoming a sort of bugbear, almost scaring many people from earnest study of
the subject as something useless.   And — what
is almost as mischievous is the way it also
presses, even upon those who do hold to faith,
who join in the old pieties of the world, and try
to keep up some little praise and prayer of their
own to the infinite goodness — but this thought,
which is in the very air of our time, comes again
and again, like a little chill of doubt.   ,

I like to say my morning prayer looking out
of the window.   Thanksgiving, to every true
heart, comes naturally anywhere — just as the
mercies of the day come to us in the common
happenings of life; but for prayer, I seem to
want as Daniel did — the open window, some
outlook on earth and sky, and all the wonderful
world, even if it may be only the grass and
flowers of some common garden, or even a tree
or two above the city roofs, — but always something of the sky and the wonderful light.   I dare
say many of you who read this feel the same —
and if you do, you will have felt how, often, the
very first thought as you look out is this wonder
of the Infinite mystery.   " Oh thou to whom I
am praying, how I long to know Thee, to know
what Thou art ! "   Thoughts of the awful vastness of this Universe, of which what one sees

is but the tiniest fragment, throng into the heart, sometimes almost dazing one. "Oh! Thou Infinite mystery, what art Thou? Art Thou such a being that Thou knowest us poor human creatures; and that I, or what I am, or what I do or suffer, or anything I am thinking or saying in my little heart of worshipping, can be anything to Thee?"

Yes, there is the unknowableness. But then comes, quickly following, almost as if it were part of the same thought — the sense that something means it all. Something "means" it. That is the word which to me seems the master-key of the perplexity. I do not say: the key out of the mystery, but, the key into it — so that it seems to open the door into the mystery, that I may look into it, and enter into it, feeling that my thoughts are not simply wandering into nothingness, but into the innermost realities of the universe, and a presence of mysterious life.

That is how the matter especially in these later years comes to me, but I am afraid that with many it is hardly so. I believe that to many in the present day that word "unknowable" has become a sort of bugbear seeming to rebuke the very faith which they still want to feel, and to make all real religion groundless and ridiculous. How, it is asked, can any one believe in that which cannot be known? How can one even attach any idea to it, or have any feeling towards it, or for it? And all this sounds plausible; and thus it happens that many people feel as if there was nothing for it but agnosticism. They would be glad if there were — but the signs seem all the other way. Instead of advancing science bringing us nearer to some knowledge on the deep subjects of faith, it seems even to be pushing them further and further away. Frederic Harrison says: " The growing weakness of religion has long been that it is being thrust inch by inch off the platform of knowledge." And, however people may regret this, they feel as if there were no resisting it, and that religion as any clear thought and strong helpful faith has to be practically left behind.

Now it is this impression that I want to do my little part to dispel. Because it is to a large extent a mere impression, and an impression partly arising from an unconscious exaggeration of the term " unknown " when applied in this realm of religion.

I think there is some help, even in the mere consideration of this difference between the part which the " unknown " plays in common life, and the part which is assumed for it in philosophy and religion. The term " unknown " is familiar

enough in daily life. Heaps of things are unknown. Great numbers of them are likely always to be so. Our knowledge even at its fur
thest and fullest, is only like a little patch of
light, which soon shades off into a limitless unknown all around us. And even the things we
talk of "knowing" in that little patch of light,
we only know partially. I know that my desk
is wood; this lamp, metal; the wall, stone — and
we can tell each other various things about each
of these substances as we call them — and we call
this knowledge. But it is only skin-deep even
with regard to the most familiar things. Different forms of matter we call them — but we
do not know what matter is — or what anything
is, in its absolute reality. Trees, flowers, or
stones that you saw in your dreams last night,
seemed just as real to you then, as these do now.
But this "unknown" is no note of hopelessness
or intellectual despair. We do not spell it with
a capital "U," or elevate the frank recognition
of it into a special class or school of thought.
We accept it as one of the conditions of our
finite, limited being, and are only thankful that
in the midst of so much that is, and is likely to
be, unknown, we can make out so much — not
perfectly, never to the ultimate fact a reality, but
sufficiently to enable us to get along tolerably

well, and to have a good practical use of the
world and of our life.

But now when we leave this common range
of visible, familiar things, and enter into the
region of Philosophy and Religion, at once the
" Unknown " begins to be regarded in quite another light.   It is put as a great thing of itself.
It must be spelled with a capital to emphasize its
importance.   " The Unknown " is talked of, as
if it were some far-away outer void, into which
no investigation could penetrate, and in ap-
proaching which, thought itself evaporates into
vague, empty, useless speculation.   The proper
recognition of this " Unknown " is elevated into
a special school of thought, and its professors
take a special name, " Agnostics," which name
has come practically to indicate those who do not
merely accept the fact of so much being Unknown, but who regard this religious part of it
as Unknowable.   That is the simple fact in the
field of human study to-day.   It is not merely
pointed out how much there is in the direction
of Religion which is unknown — but it is main-
tained that it is a direction in which knowledge
is inherently impossible, about which thought is
vain, and which ought now, among sensible people, to be put on the shelf of exploded and
abandoned ideas, like Alchemy or Astrology.

That is what I want to protest against. It is
discouraging the noblest subject of human
thought. Here in this realm of Religious Faith
is the region in which the human heart has most
longed for light, into which the human mind has
most earnestly thought and studied — and because in that direction the exact and wonderful
science of our time frankly owns that it is able
to tell us nothing, unable to find out anything,
— therefore the cry is raised " Unknown! "
" Unknowable! " and men are warned off from
it as from a mere quest among follies and delu
sions.

I do not think that this attitude will turn out
to be the real or final attitude of science. There
are many men eminent in science who altogether
repudiate any such attitude. I think it is widely
felt among the multitudes who in the present
day are eagerly studying science, and eagerly
greeting each new discovery, that while none of
the methods of science bring us into any contact
with spiritual and religious things, or even are
able to recognise such existences — yet that there
is no reason whatever for giving up belief in
them, or for ceasing to strive in other ways to
come into some realising contact with them.
There may well be other ways of penetrating
into the secrets of Universal Being than by the

microscope, or the telescope, or the marvellous
processes of chemistry! Christ's great word
that "the Pure in heart shall see God," may yet
come to be recognised — not as men generally
take it now, as a sort of shadowy parable from
real seeing, but as exact a law of spiritual perception, as Kepler's laws of Astronomical investigation are. Love, and the moral sense, and a
large part of man's best and most real life, are
equally incapable of being examined, or even
taken cognizance of, by these processes of Physical Science. Paul would say they are "spiritu-
ally discerned" — but they are very real.

I find another help in turning from the for-
bidding vastness of that term "unknown" as
it is used in religious philosophy, to its use in
the common things of life. In that Religious
Philosophy — the "Unknown" is usually treated
as absolutely unknown — nothing at all known
about it. But the moment we come back into
common life, we find ourselves talking of things,
as unknown — but hardly ever with any such
absolute meaning. In faҫt, when you come to
look naturally into it, we find ourselves conscious
of much knowledge about many things which
yet are unknown. Life is full of illustrations
of this. You find yourself in a strange room;

perhaps the occupant or owner, is some one absolutely unknown to you.   But you will not be
in that room five minutes, with an open, thought-
ful mind, without knowing something of that
unknown person.   The pictures on the walls,
the books on the table, the kind of furniture, the
very way it is disposed about the room, will tell
you something.   Or take an illustration that
struck me years ago, in one of Dr. W. B. Carpenter's essays on this very matter.   He sup
poses some one in a vast manufactory, full of all
sorts of curious and intricate workings.   This
observer traces back the power from this and
that machine, along straps, and pulleys, and
shafts — from room to room — until at last he
comes to a great blank wall, in which the shaft
disappears.   Even if you could not follow it any
further, he says, you would not conclude that
behind that wall is nothing!

Or, take a human being, — any one of the
multitudes about you.   Enough of " unknown "
and " mysterious " there, surely!   Granted it is
somebody you " know " — how much do you
know?   Who knows what man, is?   Why, this
being, which we call man, is almost as much be
yond our real ken, as God is.   The Microcosm is
as unknown as the Macrocosm!   Yet in all sorts
of ways, we find ourselves getting to know about

people, and the deep life in them, at every turn,
till we perhaps say we know them, and certainly
can love them.   And yet the wonderful human
being remains unknown; " unknowable " if you
will, but it is an unknowableness which does not
prevent all sorts of feelings of love, or hate, or
fear, and all sorts of relations of service or helpfulness.

We used to think we knew who was the author
of the 103rd Psalm — that wonderful song of
thankfulness and trust: " Bless the Lord, O my
soul, and all that is within me bless his holy
name! "   Now, we do not know, and we know
that we do not.   It is unknown, unknowable.
Yet does that Psalm the less awaken reverence,
thankfulness, trust, and lead us to the innermost
secret of human feeling?

Is it really very different from this, with regard to that infinite, " unknown " author of this
vast Universe, to whom men have all through the
ages of the world lifted up their hearts in some
kind of worship and called by some greatest name
of " God "?   God in His essence? — No, we
cannot know that, but God in his manifestations,
— is not that enough to do away with all feelings of His being some mere vast unknown abstraction?   Translate it into abstract terms if
you will.   Herbert Spencer will allow us noth-

ing more definite than this: "An Infinite and Eternal energy, from which all things proceed." This he speaks of as "the One absolute certainty." Well — that is his formula for the "unknown," but it is only half of it unknown, anyhow! "Infinite and eternal energy," yes that is unknown — but the moment you pass on to "from which all things proceed" you are in the region, not of the unknown, but of the known. I have come at last indeed to that "Blank Wall" Dr. Carpenter figured, through which I can trace no further the wonderful energy which is working through these great driving shafts which fill the world with wonderful powers and workings, evolving all things through the slowly passing cycles and periods. No, I cannot trace that Energy backwards, but I can trace it forwards, ever evolving things to something higher and nobler; from chaos to order, from the cooling star-globe to the rich earth that is about us to-day; from the rude beginnings of unconscious life to conscious man; from man only just emerging from the brute, to man with the hint of the angel in him, and the upward-reaching sense of God! "Energy," is it that only, that I may feel certain of, as Science leads me along the paths, growing every year more intricate, by which we trace the won-

derful workings in earth, air, sea, light, growth
and life? As it shows me these, and bids me
simply bow down to the " Unknowable," I cannot help replying that the energy from which
these things proceed and from which still more
proceeds the mind that studies them — and from
which proceeds also man's moral sense — and
man's strange power of love, I cannot call that
energy entirely unknown! It must be some
thing that not only causes these things to be but
means them; and the more I ponder the meaning
which comes out all through the world, and
through the mind and life of man, and through
the larger life of history, and all the world's
long struggle for truth and justice and right,
I still may not know the absolute name, but
it must be some name greater, diviner than
force or energy, some name that shall express
not how much there is that is still unknown, but
how much there is that we do know, and for
which our hearts cannot help crying out in some
glory of thanksgiving. I do not mean, that
even looked at this way, everything is clear.
There are stlll mysteries of pain and suffering
among God's works, which taken apart, do not
seem to carry any meaning of goodness in them.
The awful horrors of massacre and torture in
the East, how can God suffer such things to be,

some cry — but the nearer mystery to me, is; how can men suffer such things to be? The great meanings that have been coming out through all the slow progress of history, do come — some of them at least, visibly as the ages pass. Things grow here and there a little clearer, and I think there is a growing confidence that that vast power that is at the heart of the Universe — though still unknown — is not only a power of order, but of more than order — goodness.

So, I for one am not going to let that bugbear of the " unknown " oppress me, or drive me from the old faith which all through the best ages of man's growth has looked up with trust and adoration as to God, albeit unable to find Him out in any distinctness or perfection. As I walk through the House Beautiful of the world, I will rejoice in the sunshine, feel the awe of the storm, and bow before the wonders which make the whole more wonderful from year to year, and though I may not see the Lord of the House Beautiful, face to face, I will not call Him " unknown " I cannot but join hands with those — all the nameless multitude of souls, who through the long procession of the generations, have never seen His face yet never felt Him a mere vast unknown, but the dear presence of Infinite love and goodness. And where our vision, at times, seems very dim, there are purer and holier ones, who have seen with purer hearts, and with the faith which is more than outward sight. Let us walk with them — and most of all with the great leader of the pure in heart — let us walk with Him in his ways of prayer, trust and help ful love, and I think it will still be with us, as it has been with so many, that he will show us the Father, make very close and seal the Infinite Fatherhood, anl help us to walk and live if not yet in the light yet always towards it!

THE REALITY OF REVELATION AND AUTHORITY

In considering the great "thought-problems" — especially of Religion, a feeling besets me that our modern world — I mean the part that really thinks — is putting a little too much upon mere processes of reasoning, and especially upon what the individual can make out by such mere reasoning. So I want to put in a plea for those old-fashioned things — Revelation and Authority. Of course we have to lift those great words out of some of the old low and wrong uses of them — but still, my point is that at the heart of the idea of Revelation and also of Authority, there are great everlasting realities, which have been too much left out of late.

Thus with Revelation. Revelation has been regarded as the whole of the Bible — a certain set of Divine communications to man, dictated by the Spirit of God; and then Authority has simply meant that men are to bow down to these communications and just accept them and believe them. Now we cannot regard the Bible in any such way. To us, it is not, just as it is, a Revelation — and yet we freely speak of it as containing the records of many Revelations. And what we mean is this: the very highest and clearest discernings of religious truth in the world, have not come by the slow climbing steps of reasoning, nor as conclusions patiently built up by stage upon stage of argument. No. The very clearest and intensest discernings of Religious Truth have come in the souls of the holiest and purest not as things proved to them but rather as something shown to them, revealed in them. They have always felt that this clear light and vision was not something of their own working out, but something wrought in them or showed to them by the Spirit of God. Then, as they have told these great things to their fellow-men, men have owned them as their masters, as their teachers. And my point is, that in the working out of our religious faith, we have to allow a very large place, not an absolute authority but a very real one, to these revelations in the holiest of our race.

And let me clearly say at once that I claim a place for Revelation and Authority in Religion because I find that they have place in every other branch of human thought. My thought starts with this; we must not rest too much upon the

individual. I admit the capacity and the sacredness of the individual faculties, but that does not
involve that all individuals have equal faculties
nor that any could work out a complete religious
thought for themselves. No! such individual
ism in religion would be such a burden as man
has not to bear, does not bear, in any direction
of his thinking or investigating. There may be
no branch of study in which each man might not
possibly investigate everything and find out
everything for himself. There may be no absolute impossibility to hinder you and me from
becoming as good astronomers as those who can
predict an eclipse within 4 seconds; as good
scientists in any branch as those who are working out the wonders of biology or electricity.
But it is not likely we shall be, and certainly the
abstract possibility does not lessen the value of
their work. We listen to them as authorities.
You see we constantly use the very word in
Science, that men so kick against in Religion.
We believe, indeed, that we might verify for ourselves all they tell us. But we do not do it. We
do not think of doing it. We feel that, somehow, their faculties, though not different from
ours, have become educated to that point that
they can see things which you and I cannot see,
and we sit at their feet, are their willing and

grateful disciples. It is not an absolute authority we give them, but it is a very real au
thority. That is how the world makes progress.
What would man's astronomy amount to if each
man who was anxious about the stars had to
work out the whole subject for himself *de novo?*
What would any science amount to, if each generation started with a clean sheet? But it is
not so. " This generation seemeth a giant,"
says Lord Bacon, " because it standeth upon the
shoulders of the past." The race is bound up
together. As the ages pass, some things are
settled not to be perpetually re-opened. A few
great minds carry forward whole generations,
and teach in a year what ordinary minds could
not have made out for themselves in a century.

Now it is just the same in religion, as in
everything else. In religion, too, there is the
same help, the same rest, in the teachings of the
loftiest souls and the great accumulated convictions of mankind.

But it may be said that in all science we are
dealing not with anything akin to revelation,
truth directly perceived in the mind, but with
carefully worked out knowledge, and that we
take it because we know it has been so worked
out, and may be proved. Let us then look into
other branches of human attainment, in which

there seems a sort of direct faculty, an inner sight or sense, which cannot be proved — but which we accept because it appeals to something kindred in ourselves. And still the same principle holds. What is God's way of providing man with Art, Poetry, Music? Is it by each one being his own Artist, Poet, Musician? It would be pretty poor poetry and rather unsettled ideas of art and music we should have in that case. But no! The great Providence developes these subtle elements in man's higher nature by raising up a few who become teachers, masters, to the rest. " Masters " — no one feels any hesitation in speaking of " The Great Masters " of Art, Poetry, Music; why should we not recognise the same mastership in the Religious Life? Perhaps someone will say " Oh, but we use the word " Master " in a different way in speaking of some Musician who has given the world a new thought of Music, and in speaking for instance — of Christ. But surely it is only a difference of degree. It indicates, in each case a sort of unapproachable and inexplicable greatness which makes them our Teachers, great lights to us each in his own special realm. And there is another point of similarity in the rarity of these few greatest leaders. A friend said to me one day; " I cannot take in that idea of Christ being so unique and above all others." My answer was "How many Shakespeares have there been?" And it is a fair answer. Do you see? As you reach up among the higher faculties of Man, the great masters become fewer. And also note that their peculiar excellence is more entirely beyond the attainment of ordinary nature — a gift we call it. The great Musician's gift or the great Poet's — it is not something they slowly work out — it is a real revelation in them and they in turn become revealers to others. They do not so much touch men as reveal to them whole heights and depths of beauty, harmony, quite beyond ordinary natures. There is a perfect parallel in all these realms of study and when you look at them so, you see that it is just as natural for there to be a few mighty leaders, revealers, authorities in religion as in music or in poetry.

And mark again how exactly parallel is the relation of their higher faculties to our average faculties in both these realms. The faculties are the same in small and great, in the masters and revealers and in the multitude. There is no absolute difference between the subtle sense which makes your little child pleased with a street organ and the genius which endows a Mendelssohn or a Wagner. No absolute line divides your poetic sense which is touched by a few sweet verses, from the poetic genius which made Shakespeare. Nay — it is just because it is so, because all have something of these faculties, that those who have them in highest degree are recognised by the rest and take their thrones. Beethoven would be no king of Harmony to a race that could not even distinguish one musical tone from another. The great musicians are great, because the common race have at least music enough in them to appreciate the great ones, though not enough to be the great ones. A little poetic feeling that would not be enough to enable a man to write a line of poetry, is quite enough to feel the spell of poetry and own the great Poet, and rest in his great thoughts as a real and beautiful revelation to our hearts.

Now all this appears to be very much the same in regard to Religion. Of all the varied range of the elements and surroundings of man's being, Religion is the highest, and touches a higher influence than anything else. Its things, its relations, are all invisible; but so are the relations, harmonies, which constitute Poetry, Art, Music. Is it not reasonable, then, in man's Religious life, to expect that while the race in general shall have some feeling in the direction of religion, it shall be only a few loftiest souls here and there who are the great teachers, revealers — Masters

— to the rest? There, then, in the place and power of Revelation, in religion, as in all the higher elements of life — to lift up the dim common feeling of men into a clearer brighter light, a higher assurance, than the average humanity could ever attain for itself, and so from time to time in human history, to put in permanent authoritative shape, the great foundation truths on which man's soul may rest.

But then, some one may ask — how do we know which are the great Revealers and Authorities in the religious life? How do we know, for instance, that those old Bible leaders, and Christ at the head of them, have any such real revelation for us, in which we may feel that divine things have been made clearer for us, and to which we may look as to some reliable mastership? Our parallel still holds. You do not go casting about for proof as to who are the great masters in science, poetry, music! There is no proof. It is not even by any vote that Mendelssohn stands as a great musician, and Shakespeare as a great poet. Simply the feeling and experience of generations sifts them out, lets the small side-names and influences go, crowns the few mightiest with wreaths of light which glitter more than gold or diamonds! And so the greatest names in the religious life of mankind, stand perfectly plain. There is no mistaking them. And I do not speak of Christ alone. We are growing out of that poor conceit that the light of God never shone anywhere but in Palestine. Let us be thankful for all the great lights of the ancient world. The Vedic teachers of the original, pure Brahamism; Zoroaster; Confucius; all made Divine things clearer and more real to countless millions — real revealers in their time — and still I think it stands out more clearly to-day than ever, that there has been no religious light in the world so strong and pure as that which shines along the great Bible lines and culminates in Christ. It is not one revelation, it is a line of revelations — Law-giver and Prophet and Psalmist; not pure and absolute revelations, but very real ones, real revealings to men of brighter nobler truth from age to age, and at the head of all, the holiest, divinest life of earth — a life which though it also became overlaid with corruptions, false glorifications and all manner of superstitions, has still lived quietly on in its old simplicity in these gospels and has kept shining forth again and shines to-day, clearer, I think, than ever, still revealing the highest realities of Being, with the old and solemn certainty of a heart that dwelt in God and knew him at first hand, spirit with spirit.

I have shown then, as I think, that there is such a thing as revelation — a sort of direct perception of spiritual truth, not worked out by steps of careful reasoning, but coming like a light of God within; — and that it has been those who have had this supreme inner light who, as a fact, have been the religious leaders and teachers of mankind.

And now I want to put one or two matters touching the relation of all this to our own powers and faculties, and what should be our attitude towards it.

The special point that I want to bring out is this; that this distinct recognition of Revelation and this feeling of its authority, are not for a moment to be regarded as something that is to take the place of our own thinking and to which we are to give a blind and absolute submission. This is where I find people hesitating and perplexed. They do not seem to understand how one can speak of authority in religion, unless there is something to point to as a pure, unmixed, infallible Revelation which may be a final, absolute, authority. But that is not so. You see at once that it is not so in these other branches of human study. The great Masters are authorities — we never hesitate to speak of them as such — but their authority is not absolute. We revise our judgment of this great poet; our estimate of this musician. What we need to recognise is, that there are no final, absolute authorities in this world, on any subject. In all, we have to use the best light that comes to us from the great acknowledged teachers, and also the best light in the world's growing thoughts and faculties. And sometimes those great lights are not clear; and sometimes our own thoughts are not clear — but between them, we have to do the best we can. There is no final absolute authority on any subject — not even on Religion. The light of the world's purest religious revelations comes down to us in a Bible in which have gathered many things out of that old Hebrew life besides its Revelations. So the words and life of Christ come down to us, with some things mixed in here and there which Christ possibly never said or did! But what of that? The Bible won its place and holds its place, because, amidst whatever of earthly errors and mistakes it has, the light of God, illumining and inspiring a succession of Holy Souls and above all the soul of Christ, shines out so clear, so bright, so strong, that there is no other book like it in the world. But it is by using the light in ourselves that we find the light in the Bible. Christ's appeal was always — "He that hath ears to hear, let him hear." It was the religious nature already in them which enabled them to feel that higher religious nature in him, and to feel the power of his teaching, as he spoke to them with authority. So they heard him gladly when he gave forth the Sermon on the Mount, because they felt its truth. But they could not have composed the Sermon on the Mount. It was a real revelation to them, making the whole life of God and man clearer to them than ever before. And so it has been to men ever since, precisely because, though only a Christ could have originated it, all have power to appreciate it.

There is the power of Revelation. That which mere reasoning could not have done, that which reasoning can even find many a little fault in (sceptics pick many a hole in the great " Sermon ") has come as light to the world. Practically, the Sermon on the Mount stands at the head of the moral and religious utterances of the world. And this not for its mere details of duty, but for its great spirit of life! Life in the Will of God — God, prayer, love, eternity, — all are in it — not as the thesis of an argument, but as the light of a Revelation. And so with all the great teachings of the Bible. Do not for a moment leave even the ignorant and unlearned with the old idea that they have got to take everything in it as Divine. Teach them to read it all intelligently — but my point is that the more they do read it intelligently, the more they will feel the solemn authoritative weight with which its great testimonies of God and Duty come down through all the ages that have tried them and found them true.

And do not suppose that I would speak of those great Revelations of the past as merely a refuge for the ignorant and unlearned! Look to the quite higher range of minds, the leaders of religious movements, those who have most experienced the reality and power of religion for themselves, — George Fox, Wesley, Channing, — those who have come nearest to the Spirit of God at first hand, and so might seem to be most above any need of the help of those few greatest ones whom men have hailed as Revealers. It might seem that these would care least for any help of the Bible, and would be most impatient of any idea of sitting at the feet of Christ. But has it been so? The very opposite! Why, these have been the very ones who have prized the Bible most, most loved to study it, most laboured to elucidate it, most delighted to live their religious life in the light of its grand Psalms and Prophecies and especially in that clearest light of Christ.

Or look to the mass of average people who can think for themselves, who are thinking, and are going to think more and more: It is just this average life which is to-day most touched with the spirit of scepticism — which is largely giving up Bible reading, which is saying — "Why should we pay any special attention to what Christ said — " and which is falling back upon the individualism which says — as one said to me the other day — that in these religious things, " One man knows just as much or as little as another; and every one must just make out what he can for himself."

Well — how does this mere individualism work? It does not work at all. It lands men in mere confusion and uncertainty. Watch the common state of mind of those who thus put away all idea of any Revelation in the past. It is not that they become simply unbelievers. Nothing of the kind! Nothing so clear and definite! Simply they are all at sea. They do not know whether anything can be believed. To-day, some strong word of faith takes hold of them and they feel there must be something in it. To-morrow, they chance upon some keen argument of scepticism and they are all adrift again. Now, this curious uncertainty which is the special characteristic of to-day — what does it mean? It is the natural result of a generation which cannot indeed get quite away from its own deep down religious nature, but which is trying to grope its own way, has dropped the guiding and assuring hand of the past and cut loose from the great teachers whose clear strong sense of Divine things has for ages led the ever-growing life of mankind.

That is why I bring this subject before you. I believe that the one greatest practical need of all this restless thinking of the present day is, to be put once more in connection with its roots in the past; to cherish a more habitual sense of the significance of those long lines of gradually brightening faith which came to their brightest in Christ, to rest with quieter trust in the great religious truths to which those lines have led, and which they practically settled.

This is the help which I have found myself, and I want to help others to feel it. There have been times in my life — I dare say every one of you has experienced the same — when I needed no help, when I felt no doubt; when God and Immortality were just as plainly real to me as the sun in Heaven. Ah, if one could be always at that height! If one could fix the soul in one of those hours of clearest faith, then we might not need any help of the past, nor any more authori tative conviction than our own. But then, who can do this? With most, those hours of dear personal vision are only few and far between. There come other times when the soul strains its gaze into the surrounding mystery and can see nothing clearly, and feels as if all were doubtful. Yet, *is* all doubtful? Surely not! Is this great world of outward forms and substances less real because some are altogether blind, and many colour-blind, and the eyes of all, at times so dimmed by pain or tears, that they know not what is real? And so that great spiritual world, of Soul, and God, and Prayer, and Life beyond, is not really doubtful because the mists of doubt or sin so often cloud the inner sight or because our thoughts are sometimes dazed by the very intensity of thinking. Ah, it is then I feel the help of those old Bible pages in which the Psalmists and Prophets of the past bear witness to the ever brightening truth of God. It is there that comes in the help of him whose faith was never wavering, whose sight was never dim, and out of whose constant communion with God, came such clear, inspired certainty. Yes! In him I feel the larger life which arches over these shifting moods of Man. In him I know that it is not my times of doubt, but my times of faith that correspond to the eternal realities of things

— and resting so, sitting at the Master's feet, by and bye the times of faith come back with their new strength for life.

Mark you, it is not some minute system of doctrine, such as Theologians have worked up into their creeds that thus comes to me. I think the more I study Christ's life and word, and feel a light and power of revelation in it, the less inclined I am to try to settle all the details of belief, which yet are interesting enough in a way. But what comes to me, is, a great certainty at the foundation of things, a conviction deeper than any argument, that all that side of life is real — God, worship, duty, immortality — and that is what we all most need.

This word I am trying to say is one which seems to me to grow more and more important. Just because education is spreading, just because all subjects are canvassed and discussed as never before, perhaps since the great intellectual outbreak of the Renaissance and the great outbreak of religious thought at the Reformation — just because there is a tendency to ask for everything to be proved, is it important to remind men that in all the higher department of human nature, the best things are not susceptible of proof, do not come by argument, but rise up in the holiest souls in that " inner sight " " which is the bliss

of solitude " and so become simply " revelations " to the common world.   It has kept coming to me more and more, from my observation of the world and from my own consciousness — this sense of how we need something to rest in, something to preach from, more
strong and sure and unchanging than individual
thought — and with this the sense that we have it
— here in this Spirit and Word of Jesus Christ.
I believe that this is what the world needs to-
day.   There is a deep craving abroad for some
certainty in Religion — to know — not all the
details of Divine Realities, I think there never
was more impatience of all pretence to map out
these — but to be sure of the foundation, that
the Divine is real and man's life folded in by
Divine meaning, and moving on within the care
of infinite Love.   And this is here for us, in that
" mind of the Master " which even in our own
day has been brought out with a new clearness
and is at once the highest thought of man and
the revelation of the heart of God.   I want us
to put our hands in his and walk with him in
the ways of the spirit.   Praising God, and praying, with Him, doing all kind and helping things
we can to those about our way, with Him, and
thinking towards all further truths, to the furthest limit of our own mind and vision, and when

we fail, cleaving to him still in what discipleship we may; knowing that with that spirit, that upward look and trust, that life — with man, in God — is the secret of all ultimate truth, and the way of final light.

THE HUMAN HEART OF GOD

I TAKE this word, of the human heart of God as an expression for a divine love, compassionateness, companionship, more close and tender than any Theology has ever dared to formulate, or than any Theological term can express. I think that it was this which Christ was constantly trying to teach men. He felt how far away men were from any happy realising sense of a real fatherly companionship in their actual life. They believed in God. They believed that this great world was his creation. They believed that in the far-off past, He had come very close to Abraham and Isaac and the great patriarchs, and that Moses in the awful solitudes of Mount Sinai had heard his very words and written them down for men, for ever; and in their great Psalmists and Prophets his spirit and teaching had come into their souls with a Divine, uplifting and illuminating power. But they had no sense of anything of this kind now. The nearest they could come to it was to go to the synagogue and read how the saints of old had felt

about God, or sometimes when they were able
to visit the Temple itself to feel how in the Holy
of Holies there, God's presence was so perfect
that even the High Priest dare only enter it once
a year.　But as for Peter, when he was sitting
mending his nets and getting ready for a night's
fishing, having any feelings of God being with
him, or that it would be a pleasant sense of companionship to think of Him so — or as for
Peter's wife, in the midst of her house-work or
when the bed-ridden mother who lived with them
was cross or impatient, just resting her heart in
the thought of the Heavenly Father being there
with her and sympathising with her — why, they
did not feel like that, or think of it as the thing
to feel.　And that was what Jesus did feel, and
wanted all men to feel, and what he preached in
his gospel, or " good news," and tried to draw
men to him to shew them, and to make them see
it and feel it, as he did.　For he could not help
feeling that if he only could get men close to
him, and believing in him so that he could open
his heart to them, they also would see God and
feel this Fatherhood in everything, and in their
own hearts, even as he did.　That is how that
word comes in so closely to his thought, " If ye
had known me ye should have known my Father
also!"　It was a word to his disciples, who had

come to him, and been with him, and thought they knew him, but yet had been half blinded to all his deeper meaning by their thought — which they still kept clinging to — of his going to be their King.

The Human Heart of God: As one tries to realise this, as what Christ wanted to teach others, because he so felt it himself, the thought arises — How came he to feel it so? Why, that saying — "If ye had known me, ye should have known my father also," seems so high, so above what any human being could say, that some doubt whether he ever did say it, whether it was not some mere gloss or addition of the writer of this gospel; or, if Jesus did say it, whether it would not tend to prove that he felt himself God, as after ages made him out to be. But in reality there is not a shadow of such a meaning in it! All through, he is trying to direct men's thoughts to the One Infinite God whom his people had always believed in, but whom they had put so far away; he is trying to bring their thought of that Infinite God from the far-off inaccessibility in which they had been thinking of Him. "It is He that sitteth upon the circle of the earth and the inhabitants thereof are as grasshoppers!" That was the kind of saying that the Hebrew mind dwelt upon. It was along that line that

the Rabbinical Schools felt their way towards
the Divine. But it was not in the Rabbinical
schools that Jesus found Him. He made out the
heart of God from his own heart. It was
knowledge of God at first hand. One cannot
help thinking that it came first of Mary's
mother-teaching, that this first opened the child
heart to the great, almost forgotten reality of
God's close presence, and that so came that
watching and waiting of the pure, open soul, to
which gradually were borne in impressions, dis-
cernments, impulses, which revealed themselves
to him as the working of the Divine in him.
Does any one ask how much was of himself and
how much of the spirit of God? Who can ever
say, in any of the great revelations of high truth
and holy presence, that have lighted up the path
of man's uplooking through the ages with a light
above man's own. But here and there in his utterances of this reciprocal consciousness, you
catch some glimpse of how he felt it. "Believe
me that I am in the Father and the Father in
me!" "The words that I speak unto you, I
speak not of myself," and, highest of all: "I
and my father are one!" In all his best life he
felt that Divine companionship, that it was not
just he himself thinking and feeling, but he and
God, thinking, feeling, together — and especially

the very highest thought, the very tenderest feeling, that in which he most seemed lifted out of
self and above self — *that,* God's. Certainly it
was a very exalted feeling — and it is not strange
that those who had not come anywhere near this
feeling misunderstood him. I do not wonder
that the sharp rabbinical critics of Jerusalem —
steeped to the eyes in technicalities and formalism — when they heard him talk that way, cried
out that he was "blaspheming" and "making
himself out to be God!" I do not wonder that
the most even of his disciples retained very little
of that side of his teaching (of his close life with
God) in their remembrance; and that even John,
who had the tenderest sympathy with that deepest side of Christ, and remembered most of it,
did not always remember it quite clearly, and
still further failed to transmit it clearly to his
followers; so that in these gathered recollections
of his teachings which give us John's teaching
of the Gospel, there are dark and perplexing
sayings, as well as these exceedingly bright ones.
And so again, I do not wonder that at a still
later time when Christian faith had cooled down,
quite away from any living realisation of
Christ's feeling, men said straight out that he
must have been God to have spoken so. And
still, as I read and read, I know that all that

Deification is a mistake, and a mistake that has taken men away from Christ's real thought and feeling, and from the very thing he was trying to do. For that thing he was always trying to do, was to lift all men with him, into the same sense of the Father's nearness — " He is in you also," he said. " He will be with you." And as clear as his word of his being one with this indwelling spirit of God, is his great prayer that his disciples also might be One, in that same oneness! And though he never used the expression of " The Human Heart of God," yet the phrases that he did use have been so much formalised and spoiled that this comes to me as about the freshest and most living phrase for that sense of close, divine companionship and sympathy which Christ so felt and wanted all to feel.

The Human Heart of God. Now, from trying to make out that highest way in which Christ felt this, let us come down to our own poorer and duller life and see what help it has for us. Why, to begin with, it starts us in our seeking for God at a nearer, more hopeful, point. " Feeling after God, if haply we may find him — " I suppose that is one of the old Bible words which most come home to our common experience.

We long to know God more closely. For we know God is — must be, and if he were not anything to which we feel able to give such a personal name, still there must be some Divine equivalent, even if it is only what Herbert Spencer calls the " Infinite energy that sustains all things." But whatever it is, or He is, how we do feel after it for some clear touch or thought or apprehension of that highest mystery. But we are always beginning at the wrong end! We begin with the abstract, with vast, far-away thoughts of Infinitude, or something as near Infinitude as we can think. We think of the vast spaces of the Infinite Heaven of worlds; and consider if we can fill them up with some conception of Being that could have any thought or care for us little insects of a day on this smallest of the sky's hinted worlds. And we cannot make much of it that way — nay, when we think out into those vast infinitudes, instead of finding much help to faith in God there, we have to take a pretty strong clear faith with us there, or we shall find nothing. Or again, we work along the thought of the moral — which is so much grander than the material — but still we are apt to start from the abstract. We begin by trying to imagine the Divine Perfection. That is where all the great theologies into which men have tried to systematize Christianity, have begun. They have begun with that far-off, abstract perfectness. God is there; that is God; and Man ought to be there, and if man is palpably not there, that is man's own fault and sin, explained this way or that. That abstract Divine perfectness is the sort of fixed point, by which, from which, all things are measured, and man put, (in his own thinking) almost hopelessly away from God.

It is true that these same Theologies, having thus started their systems with Man infinitely far away from God, have then proceeded to elaborate certain complicated systems for bringing him near again; and in all those systems Christ is brought in, as somehow bringing these two infinitely separated things (God and Man) together, on certain conditions, always, — of faith, or works, or by a certain sacramental process duly gone through. But all these things seem to me to miss the great essential thought of the heart of Christ. That thought is, through out, of God's present love — God near to all — loving all — not just going to love them when they have been converted or changed and brought, somehow, near to Him, but loving them now, the sinner, the outcast, man even in the most elementary stage, even in his lowest sav-

agism even in his furthest lapses into sin. Yes
— God not loving sin — but understanding sin,
not averted by it, pitying it, patient with it. The
human heart of God. Yes — anything is better
than that abstract thought of the Divine Heart
(of the theologian) in its passionless perfection,
turned all away from the common world's poor
worldly living, and only in any close communion
with pure souls in their most elevated moods.
Nay, I would sooner follow the common human
heart in all the familiar working of its interests,
admirations and affections. They may seem
small enough as they come out in any single life
with its poor little limitations, and yet they may
touch us with glimpses of a sort of divine meaning
and suggestions of infinite possibilities. Here is
a poor woman, " fussing among her plants " as
her neighbours and children say—loving them,
loving them like little children, putting this one
in more sunshine, that into the shade, washing
off the blight and scale, watching each new bud —
such hope and such sorrow when the bud does
not come to a good flower but seems somehow to
dry up and wither. That woman, with her loving care for this infinitesimal fraction of the
mighty world, is but a very small item in the
forces which are the outcome of the infinite sustaining energy that we call " God." Yet, as I

follow this thought of the Human Heart of God,
I seem to get a new glimpse of what all the
mighty evolution of things means. Mr. R. A.
Armstrong, in his book " God and the Soul " (to
my mind one of the best and most helpful books
of the day) gives us as a phrase for the omni-
present life of God in the world, this: " Attention concentrated everywhere." Only let us add
to this " Love." " Loving attention." You know,
so long as you have to conceive of one " infinite
sustaining energy " in and through all things, it
is no harder really to conceive of that " Infinite
energy," that cosmic force, as love, also; it is
only beginning at the human end of the vast
force and having the courage of the thought. Begin, as I have said—not with the gravitation (of
which we really know nothing) with which the
Infinite Energy works among, the vasts of space,
but with the loving care of a woman among her
flowers. She and her flowers of which we know
a good deal, are just as much outcomes of that
Infinite Divine energy, as gravitation is — of
which we know nothing. But begin here and
even that little sense of human care and love en-
larges into a sweet companion thought of Divine
love and care, the shadow of a sweet presence.
And when with that sweet companion thought
and presence, you go among all the variety of

human doings, I do not say it makes all plain, but here and there it touches things with little lights of interpretation which seem to come out of the meaning of the whole, which shew me the trend of the whole, and which help me to trust even where I cannot see. I see a true teacher among his boys, true parents among their children, trying harder than ever that woman works among her plants to train them up into good, happy, wholesome childhood, and so still on into good, wholesome, manhood and womanhood. Of course it is not a perfect trying anywhere and the results are just as imperfect, often dreadfully disappointing. The children don't grow straight, the men and women come up into poor stunted half lives — but all the process and all our disappointment at the poor result points to something higher; and all our sense of impotence and failure does not excuse itself but finds a certain rest in the thought of the human heart of God!

And so it may be, too, when it is we ourselves who are the failures. I think the most pathetic thing in all this complicated Universe is its moral struggle. We conceive such high ideals and we fall in actual living so pitifully below them. Here is a man with, as Burns wrote of himself "passions wild and strong." Perhaps he has many noble thoughts of life, but he yields to the tempta-

tions; then he is ashamed and despondent.   In
that shame he feels as if God could have no joy
in him, no love for him, could only regard him as
a hypocrite and resent any thanksgiving and
prayers from him as lies and insults.   It may not
be so bad with you, but we all know something of
what it is.   For an outburst of angry temper or
one mean piece of selfishness, may sweep away
all our piety and make us ashamed of the good we
have thought of but have let go.   We feel afraid
to look into the face of God—what is that perfect
holiness to us?   We are afraid to worship, afraid
to think of him as near us.   But when this
thought comes to me of the Human Heart of
God, I do not feel that it makes any wrong doing less, but it does help me still to cling to God,
and not utterly to despair.   One hesitates perhaps
to think much about it for oneself, for fear of
seeming to excuse oneself, but for all the poor
weak sinning of the world it comes as such a
light and help.   Why are we to be impatient or
despairing because people are only at the poor
beginnings of that ideal goodness towards which
God is leading on His world?   The world is only
at the beginning of it!   Even the best, most advanced part of the world, is only at the beginning
of the real highest life, as we see it shadowed
forth to us in the noblest.   And down among the

least advanced, the lowest races of the world, we can but grope about with our thoughts of evolution and a dim sense of the measureless ages through which we have been brought even to where we are. But surely it has been a power working towards good, and meaning the good, that has been leading all on, and is leading all on still to heights far above our noblest actual, in which Christ lives, in the very heart of the Eternal; interpreting that heart of God to the heart of man, in Love. That is why Christianity lays such supreme stress on love. True, it puts righteousness in all sorts of flashing lights of meaning and attractiveness, and sometimes of awe and fear lest we should lose it—but over all love, for love is the power that really lifts man up, making some finer greatness than he has, beautiful and ad mirable to him, so that he longs for it and is stirred by it to loyalty, imitation, self surrender. And so, through the human heart of man, climbing a little toward higher things through the long dim past, and through that highest human heart which Christ has shewn us in himself and in our best self, through all this we get some sense of the Human Heart of God. And when once we have got this thought and clasped it to us, — I do not say it makes all things plain, but it does touch with some new lights of meaning and trust, alike the long, dim past, and the confused and tangled present — and the vast, vague eternity beyond. And here, in this little fragment of the whole, where we are struggling on, to-day, it helps us to rest in God a little more confidently, and even through all shame of weakness and failure and sin, to know that we are still in His heart of meaning, and that nothing can separate us from the Love of God.

THE FOREORDINATION OF GOD

THERE is a truth in these words which is too much left out in our modern religious thinking, and to which I want to draw your attention. " Foreknowledge," " Foreordination," " Predestination,"—they all refer essentially to the same thought, and it is a thought which the Liberalism of to-day rather shrinks from. This is the day of self-reliance. Man's nature and power are magnified more than ever before. And yet, when this exuberant feeling of freedom has done its most and its best, man finds himself constantly confronted, stopped by facts, tendencies, forces against which he is powerless, and which if this universe is a universe of orderly meaning, mean another larger will than ours. In man's religious thinking he has called this " the foreordination of God "—I like that word for it best. It is a deep subject, touching on one side the highest questions of metaphysics and philosophy; and as such it might seem beyond the scope of our consideration here. But then, it is a subject which on the hither-side touches every alternative of our daily living, our thoughts of duty, our struggles after righteousness, everything on which moral life depends, and so we have to have some thought about it; and it may be helpful to see some of the great thoughts of men about it, and especially to see what were the real thoughts of the Gospel men and times.

Perhaps in the forefront of the world's thought on the subject of God's foreordination stands Calvinism. Calvinism was based entirely on God's foreordination, and carried out the thought with a rigid and remorseless literalism, as if foreordination, was the whole truth, and the one absolute equation of man's life and destiny. It did not do so at the beginning. It is often forgotten what a noble rebound of real faith Cal vinism was in its beginning. You see, in the middle ages, Religion had more and more come to be summed up in Purgatory. The popular religion of the middle ages concentrated its real force and interest on Heaven, and Hell, and especially on Purgatory. You see the intensity of its interest, in Art, Literature; the pictures of Judgment, the Epics of Dante, Purgatory occupied the whole horizon of thought. The Reformation tore all that away; all that higgling of Priests about indulgences, all that apparatus of masses and prayers for the dead. The Reformation tore all

that away, and threw men back on—what? On
the foreordination of God! God has settled all
that beforehand—in the mighty sweep of his
world-plan. He hasn't left it to be bargained over
by the priest's masses or Tetzel's indulgences. It
is all settled—if for Heaven, then "Glory be to
God"; if for Hell, still not ours to dispute it,
"Glory be to God."

Leave all that eternal future in God's settlement
of it, and, now, go to work, here in this present
world, where God is calling us to do His present
will, and to set up His present kingdom! That
was the spirit of the first Calvinism; and what a
deliverance it was to feel that all that eternal
future was out of their hand or care, history
shows. Probably nothing could have done away
with all that peddling and fussing about the future, except that strong, simple truth, even so im-
perfectly conceived as it was, of the Foreordination of God. And if men had left it there, simply
as a great rock of trust in the background of
their thought, it would have been well. But they
could not leave it there. By and bye theorizing
began, and the wire-drawing of logic. All souls
foreordained to Heaven or Hell before they were
born? The moment men began to look closely
into that, all sorts of difficulties arose. What of
infants, dying before they were old enough to

have done either right, or wrong, it seemed as if foreordination must involve Infants being in Hell! Then, in another direction; if all that eternal future is settled by Divine decree irrespective of life or character, what can it matter whether one's life be good or bad, and foreordination, carried to that extreme, landed men in the moral chaos of Antinomianism.

Well, Calvinism had its day, a strong day, during the fighting and struggling time of the Reformation; for it was a grim time, and it needed an iron creed to carry men through; but when it came to a religion simply for common living, it would not do. It had been clamped and bolted together, well, with numberless texts, but the natural heart and conscience were too strong for it. Men could not believe in a God—sending

— — —" Ane to Heaven and ten to Hell
　" A' for thy glory,
" And nae for ony guid or ill
　" They've done afore ye."

All sorts of schemes, of semi-Calvinism and so forth were attempted, but finally it has practically disappeared; only the trouble is that it has left behind it a prejudice against the whole thought of foreordination, whereas, as I have said, that is a truth based in the very reality of things and not to be let go without loss and harm to all true religious life.

The trouble with Calvinism's setting forth of foreordination was that it took it as if it were the whole of truth, and worked from it with the rigid literalism which has exaggerated and defaced so many of the Bible words.

In reality one great thought runs through the Bible, through the whole of the old Hebrew history—not equally felt at all times or by all, but aways coming up again—and illuminating their whole history. That thought was, of a great purpose of God, to be worked out in men, and to be worked out by them. Yes, "by" them— always the thought of their part went along with the greater dominating thought of God's purpose. Their part might fail. "Who hath believed our report?" cried the greatest of their prophets. They might be unfaithful to God's trust, then would it be given to others to fulfil; but fulfilled it would surely be! This was "Foreordination" as it grew up in the mind of Israel, nothing to do with man's eternal personal destiny, to which Calvinism especially applied it, but the thought of a great Divine plan and purpose running through the ages. And when you come to the development of it, in the thought of Christ and Paul and the early Christians, you see at once what a tremendous strength it gave them. Their whole work was done in the great sense, that they were not the mere opportunists of a new religious movement, but the agents of God's providence, carrying on a work which had been in the eternal mind from the beginning of the world!

You see this in Christ himself. We are not to think of him as of some casual reformer, who saw formalism and ceremonialism lording it over the people and who rose up to denounce them. The thought of the great work his people might be doing for the truth of God possessed his soul. "Ye are the light of the world," he said! In stead, they were hiding it under a bushel; it was upon his soul to lift it up, to inspire his people with the ancient thought of the glory of it, and to lead them into a new life of showing it to the world! The Jews upbraided him as an upstart, an ignorant, unauthorised Galilean setting his word against all their ancient law and way. "The word that I speak unto you, I speak not of myself!" was his reply. They quoted Abraham. "Abraham saw my day and was glad" — the "teaching of Abraham carried in its heart this Gospel I am giving you." They mocked. "Thou art not yet fifty years old, and hast thou seen Abraham?" But he was speaking not of personal things but of that great movement of pure religion of which he saw the beginning in Abraham, and felt the later inspiration in himself — and all, Abraham, and He, alike the agents of that great foreordination. "Before Abraham was, I am" was his great word. People have taken that — the Jews took it — as an assertion of personal pre-existence, but that was only a clumsy lowering of his thought. He was plainly speaking of this great claim of the divine education of the world, and asserting his own place as a link in it, and all in the mind of God from the beginning. That is the thought he loved to fall back upon — that was what he meant by his "Messiahship," that he was fulfilling a great purpose of God which was from the foundation of the world. That was his strength and glory. That is what he prayed might more and more appear. "Now, O Father, glorify me with that glory which was before the worlds!" It was no cheap, personal ambition, but his confident prayer for the outshining of that divine light and truth which at the moment seemed to be rejected and despised.

That this was the meaning in the Master's heart we are confirmed in feeling, by seeing how the Apostles took it in, and dwelt on it, as one of the most uplifting thoughts of their own ministry. For the same obloquy which assailed their master assailed them still more. Who were they, ignorant upstarts contradicting the ancient things, and preaching a Christ whose claim had been manifestly disallowed by God, disproved by the shameful ending of the cross? Realise that, and then you will understand the strength they found in falling back upon the foreordina- tion of God, and how this grew into one of the great stock thoughts of their preaching. They were nothing in themselves, but in Christ they were part of God's meaning and purpose from the foundation of the world. They were not dis- couraged by the crucifixion. If the Jews " by wicked hands " had crucified him, it was " by the determinate counsel and foreknowledge of God " that he had been " delivered up." He was " the lamb that was slain from the founda- tion of the world "; that saying alone should be enough to take away any idea of personal pre- existence from these allusions, the whole thought was, of all as in the mind of God, from the beginning.

This great thought lifted them above all fail ure. And so they used it to overcome the dis- trust, the fears, the weakness of their followers. " God hath chosen us in him, before the foundation of the world, having predestined us by the adoption of children."

Hence the tone of glad assurance and encouragement that rings through those early Christian writings. " Ye are the elect of God!" " God hath called you "; " he hath predestined you," to this new life in Christ! Think with what force and help such words would come to those poor labourers in Rome or Corinth — water-carriers and quarry-men, and humblest folk, who before had lived on from day to day with no thought that any God in Heaven or Earth cared for them, or wanted them. "God wants you!" He wants even you to help Him in this mighty world-plan for the salvation of mankind — and not them alone, so God wanted all men, called all men! Grand words of assurance and encouragement, and always leaving place for personal effort, but personal effort based upon the sense of a great divine impulse and leading, which foreordains the good, and asks for our help, but will surely fulfill, even if we fail or turn aside.

There is the great difference between Foreordination as a doctrine in Calvinism, and fore-ordination as a great assurance of Faith, in the New Testament. Calvinism took these great assurances of Faith and treated them as so many exact propositions of theological science, and then with the rigid literalism which has spoiled so many of the grand old Bible sayings, it worked them up into a categorical system of everything being exactly and unchangingly foreseen for all eternity. No room for possibility of change, no room for man's free action. But in reality, the old Bible words which thus were treated as exact theological propositions, were nothing of the kind! Paul was not writing theology, or shaping out systems. He was writing strengthening letters to weak men and women, just assuring them that God had need of them, wanted even their help and witness in His mighty plan; and really in his strongest utterances of Divine plan and will, appealing for man's help to be given freely.

It is that old truth of Foreordination, not as Calvinism disfigured and narrowed it, but as it lay as a great faith in the heart of Christ and Paul and that earliest Christian time; it is that old truth of a Divine purpose and power in the world leading things on, that we want to bring back a little more into our religious faith. We are still too apt to feel as if we, and all the works and institutions of the world, were mere casual incidents in a vast order of things — sometimes it almost looks to us like a vast disorder — in which we have to do the best we can, now for each other, or for some seeming good of the whole. Yet our very science, our study of outward nature, might teach us better. No lack of a long, slowly working order there! I think it was Huxley who used to say " there is a great deal of Calvinism in nature." Through what seems, looked at in detail, infinite variety, confusion sometimes almost to caprice, we get continual glimpses of a vast world-order, slowly, remorselessly working itself out. Nay, not " working itself " out. If it were simply one continually repeated grind, the same order over and over again, then it might conceivably be that — but a vast world-order that has constant progress in it, from fire mist to circling spheres, from circling spheres to worlds — one of them at least, grassing over, developing life — life still in orderly, upward progress, from monad up to man — from man in the mere bones and muscle and passion of the savage, to man in the brain and conscience and heart of the sage or Saint? Is there no foreordination there? Is all this wonderful creation something that has taken this form, or that, haphazard, and at last stumbled into man? And then, onward still, stumbled into human progress, and into the great personalities of history? Did not the Almighty mind mean " man " from the beginning? Is it not Foreordination all along the line of evolution? Is not evolution indeed, merely the scientific name for that great Foreordination? " Thou lovedst me from the foundation of the world," said Christ in his prayer, and it has seemed to men an awful word to have said, but is it not really true of every son of man? In that great plan for the leading on of man towards truth, towards goodness, towards all nobler life, does not God love his Christ's only? Is not every soul that shares their service, called to it, and dear to the Infinite heart? And what a strength is in that thought for all who dare to share, however humbly, in doing any little work that may make the world a better, happier place! Look at it how you will, the thought is an uplifting one. The poet's dream of " One far off divine event, to which the whole creation moves " — nay, it is not a mere dream, say rather a vision of the uplifted soul!

Of course one cannot outline it all exactly and say, in all the busy turmoil of our doings, how much is the foreordination of God, and how much the contribution of man's free will, or how (if God has foreordained anything) man can really have any free part. And man can go on puzzling, indeed men have done ever since they began to think of such things at all, puzzling themselves to reconcile the two — God's foreknowledge, and man's freedom. Perhaps man's logic never will reconcile the two, but man's life has to reconcile them every day; and all good, earnest life, living to any large thought of duty, and trying to be on the side of the world's forces of good, loses all difficulty — works not as one bound or fettered, but with a gladder and more eager freedom because feeling that the world's forces of good, are foreordained of God, and foreordained to conquer in the end. I remember James Freeman Clarke speaking of how this came to those who like himself had struggled (through the great Civil War in America) to lift that war above mere politics and keep it true to its greater issues of freedom. He said that for long, they seemed to be struggling alone, all in confusion, but as the end drew on, the greater meanings seemed to clear themselves — and when the great events came, one by one, the abolition of slavery, the Fall of Richmond, the close of the war — he said — they felt as if these were not their doing, but "came like things foreordained from the foundation of the world."

No! Once more, it is not a *doctrine* I am arguing to prove; but, that we take in, a little more, into our hearts and lives the thought of the Divine meanings, working themselves out in human history, and the divine meanings that are always in the world, mutely appealing to us all to take hold and keep them on! Not ours perhaps to see exactly what the end shall be — not ours at all to see the final victory — but ours to press on in the direction of the light, doing all helpfulness and kindness as we march along, and feeling that the ways of God though slow are sure, sure from the foundation of the world, sure into the far recesses of eternity.

THE HEALING FORCES OF GOD

THE healing forces in Nature, and especially the quiet way in which they seem to work; — that is the thought suggested to me by the old gospel story — of the poor infirm man healed at the Pool of Bethesda and not knowing who had healed him. Destruction is often sudden enough both in nature and in human history, but healing and restoration so often work quietly and silently. I do not give it as any new idea, but it is one of those old thoughts which is well worth following out a little, not only as a curious matter of observation — but as a thought with help and truth in it, a thought to bring us nearer to the Infinite Life that works in this beautiful silent way, — and also to help us to do our part, and to be content to do it, more in the same quiet way.

Look at the healing work in Nature. The lower down you begin, the more visibly striking it is. In the very lowest forms of life you often see them seemingly destroyed in some essential, but nature grows on a new part, and quietly makes

them right again.   Here and there you pick up
a star-fish on the sand, that has thus had one of
its tentacles broken off and grown again.   Watch
the boat-man going his round among his lobster-
pots and here and there it is a lobster or a crab
that has thus lost a claw, and had it restored —
a little smaller than the original one, but still
a serviceable limb.   You break a twig, or even
a bough, off a tree; and something begins silently
to heal the scar, and in doing so to make up
for the loss by some new growth all about.   You
cannot actually see those quiet restorative processes by which Nature thus begins to make all
right again.   You may watch, but it is like a
child watching the hour-hand of the clock, or
the shadow of the sun — it gets from point to
point, but you cannot see the movement.   You can
see the lightning-flash — but you can not see
the electricity accumulating.   So on a larger scale.
You wound the green surface of the earth with
spade or plough; you pile the fiery slag-heaps
from the furnace upon the fields, or disfigure
the valley side with the great bare cutting or
embankment of your railroad.   Quietly, silently,
the healing forces of God go to work to make
all right again.   The winds are His messengers.
The birds carry seeds for Him.   The very earth
worms do their humble service.   In a little while,

the raw furrows show a sheen of vegetation;
the scarpment of the railroad is grassing over;
the very slag-heaps shew here and there a weed,
and by and by whole patches of greenery. It
makes one feel as if the whole atmosphere must
be full of spores and seeds, waiting for any place
where they may find the chance to grow. You
call them weeds perhaps, though, bear in mind,
the more you know of them, the less inclined
you will be to call them so; and the real botanist
prizes every little meanest one of them, and gives
it a respectful Latin name, and stores it among
his treasures. And the Lord cares for them all,
for these also are a part of His ways, and thus
" He reneweth the face of the earth."

Or, come up higher. Look at all this in these
bodies of ours. You cut your finger: you can
see and feel that. But who can see the actual
working of the process, by which it heals again.
You talk of granulation and the formation of
tiny cells one from another, and so forth. True,
but that is only the merest outside of the matter, and there your knowledge stops. Often you
cannot tell even so much. Here is a poor woman
lying sick and ill in a room that since she lay
there has grown littered and dirty, with foul bad
air, and children messing about; and the doctor
comes, and reads the story at a glance, — hard

work, poor food; — for what medicine can do, gives such remedy as he can, at least to help things, and as he will say to you, to give nature a chance — but "he will ask the district nurse to call." Ah, there is some help! — a kind woman's face; a deft womanly hand, making some kind of a pillow, straightening things out a little, encouraging the eldest child to do what she can; opening the window, sponging the hot face and grimy hands; and shewing the neighbor-body loitering helplessly about, half a dozen little things that any one can do, once shewn how; why when the nurse goes away to some other poor sufferer, even before the little morsel of nicely cooked food that she will perhaps send, is come, the poor woman feels the room a sweeter place, and can be more patient with the children, and feels in herself, a new hope of getting well again, — and a cheery thought, perhaps, of how that little room might be a brighter place than for a long time past she has had spirit to make it.

Or, you take an ailing, drooping child out of the close, bad air of some poor court, away to the seaside or the open hills; and gradually the thin little limbs fill out, and the pale face shews a new colour, and the listless, feeble voice is shouting with the children at play. What is it? Who has done it? Somebody will tell you perhaps that it is the "ozone" in the air. But how far in, does that go to any real explanation? It may be true as far as it does go — but how far in is that? The Psalmist did not know much about ozone — but his thought about such things, was — "Bless the Lord, O my soul, and forget not all his benefits! who healeth all thy diseases, who redeemeth thy life from destruction; who crowneth thee with loving-kindness and tender mercy!" I do not see why the two thoughts should not go together. For they belong together. That is why I have put as my subject the healing forces of God. Of Nature, if you will, certainly — or rather in Nature — ; but that only sends us to outward phenomena, and trains of carefully observed cause and effect, and we are soon at the end of all we know, or are likely to know. Do not let even that little that we observe in the outward order be despised. The true thought reaches all the way from the vast invisible life that we call God, to the visible life and form of outward Nature. As Tennyson says —

"If He thunder by Law, the thunder is yet His voice" and if we find out the law of the thunder, still God is there; and so if we find out the law of our healing, still God is there. The true thought will keep the two things together, all the outward fact and law that we can observe, and all the Divine meaning and Will, to which, (with however long a gap in our tracing), our observation leads us back. So we have to include in grateful reverence not only all our faith in the soul and God, but the outward body and the natural world, and all the science and all the law that are stored in the chemist's shelves, or in the Physician's brain. There is the essential shallowness of this latest fad which calls itself " Christian science," but which is really as far from Christianity as from science. It entirely dissociates the outward fact and law, from the inward spiritual and divine. It treats the outward order, with its disorders which are only another side of the order, as nothing — mere evil illusion, the belief that they are *anything* being in fact the only real disease! We are to think ourselves part of God. The one formula for all outward ailment — or what we *think* outward ailment, is, to become absolutely possessed with the omnipresence and love of God!

The extravagance is all the sadder because it borders upon the deepest truth, but taking in that alone, and out of all proportion, not only makes itself ridiculous, and tends to set people against it. For God is in all things; and in the make-up of our complex human being Mind is King. Among the " healing forces of God," are faith, and happy trust, and man's own will — these are part — but to treat any of them as all, is just " the falsehood of extremes." After all, the body, also, is the Lord's, and fearfully and wonderfully made; and its laws also are " parts of His ways." So let man study reverently the Physical laws, the laws of bodily health among them — and follow them out and make the best of them. Only, let these thoughts of law and knowledge lie in man's mind, folded in the vaster thought which we call God.

I said that all this is a thought of Trust. And I think it is. Knowledge is something — yes, is much — and yet when we have followed it the best and closest that we can, it goes such a little way, after all, back into the real nature of things; but as it shades away out of our sight, it shades off, not into nothingness or a mere confusion of half-seen facts and fancies, but into a mystery of dimly discerned life and will, and of vast, hinted meanings.

Among those hinted meanings is this which all that I have said leads up to: A sort of healing impulse seems to be part of the Animating force of Nature. It is not a little detail of Zoology or Botany. It seems part of the principle of things — a silent tendency towards order, beauty, life. The original force of evolution, in spite of some reversions here and there is quietly onward. You may not see it to-day; but look at the universe of the primal fire-mists and compare it with the universe into which it has grown, to-day, and the onward tendency is unmistakable — and the more you allow for the occasional cataclysms which mark off the cosmic periods, and have seemed so destructive, the more you are impressed with the silent restorative and healing forces which have kept renewing the face of the world. We have to take in that, as the background of all our studies of the ways of things in Nature, and of all our endeavours to do any healing we can, ourselves. And it is a great thought of trust. Man, in his attempts at healing, however poor they may be, is helping the great meanings of God. And he will do his healing part the better, more con fident when on the right track, and less dis mayed by sometimes failures,— if he remembers this great truth and thinks of it —" God's Healing forces."

I think it is *here* that the story of Christ always has a meaning in the world's life, beyond that of any private individual of this or that time, however wise and good. It seems as if that

overmastering sense of sonship and of working
with the indwelling spirit of God — something
which all God's children might have and which
he longed for all to have — but oh how few had it,
or even dream of what it might be — was to him,
life's great reality. And it seems as if that lifted
him into a real leadership and Lordship over
the thought and life of man. And in nothing
was this more striking, than in his ministry
and proclamation of new life to men. Life, hope,
blessing and all healing, in the new life of men,
in the love of God and of one another — that
was the essence of his gospel. The world seemed
a crushed, crippled world to him. Among his
own people their very religion, seemed rather
to be crushing men, than uplifting them. In
that old light of the Law, all life lay burdened
by judgment. All disease, especially, was judgment for some sin, even if men did not know
what. That thought crushed the fresh energy
which might have striven for health. Such ef
fort would seem mere useless writhing against
the decrees. It was not the mere sickness, it
was this crushed, hopeless condition that called
Jesus forth. With his heart full of the sense of
the life-giving presence and love of God, it
seemed as if the very message of that would
be blessing and healing to the world. How much

the spring and power of that message had to do with all that healing that we read of, and with all the impression of healing power in him which irradiates the Gospel story, who shall say? Simply it seems as if, wherever he came, something of a new life, and with it a new gladness of health, pulsed through the multitudes who gathered around him. And some explain it one way, some another; " faith," " power of mind over matter "; — and some — among whom I claim a place — do not explain it, simple accepting Christ's feeling about it which found God's power in the forefront of it, himself only the humble instrument.

But it is with regard to the higher moral and spiritual healings, that the thought of the man not knowing who had healed him, comes with deepest suggestiveness. Christ's miracles of healing are always going on — though now people say: " it is only the healing of the soul." Only? as if there was any healing in the world to compare with that of turning a man from evil to good, and helping him to keep on trying and trying again, until he is a changed man. That was the greatest wonder in the old time. So quietly he came, unnoticed in the crowding of history: — a Syrian peasant, — which was all men saw of him, a Syrian peasant — musing

on the Salvation of the world. And for a year
or two he preached the new life among the people, and then he passed away out of sight, as he
did that day from the pool of Bethesda. But
when he left the world, he left it different from
what he found it; — new seeds were growing
in it, new forces; the blind soul saw, the par-
alysed will rose up and walked, the crippled life
of man stood upright on its feet. And yet so
quietly did the blessing come, so little with any
" observation," that it was as the old word says:
" He that was healed wist not who it was."
They thought — that was the form their wonder
grew into — that it must have been God himself
who had come down and wrought such blessing.
They did not know the imperishable power there
is in simple human goodness working in love of
God and man; in a simple human soul raised to its
highest power by the felt indwelling of the spirit.
But then, since Christ shewed men how, the healing work of his life and spirit has been repeated
all along the ages — and always in the same
quiet way. Mostly men have not recognised it.
They have set up their great hierarchies, shak-
ing the earth with the tread of their power, and
asserting themselves to be the only channels of
healing mercy to mankind, the representatives of
Christ on earth. And the healing work has gone

on, yet not much through them. But always, up and down the world, there have been quiet faithful hearts which have caught the master's spirit and have touched with that spirit the works and cares, the sorrows and the sicknesses of men. The world is touched to-day with a humaner spirit than, I think, ever before. Often it hardly knows from whom the healing comes. It is some one close about, a long way nearer than that Jesus of eighteen hundred years ago, who gets a hold on his fellow-clerk or workmate and sets him feeling that life might be a better thing; wins him into this class or meeting, or that little work of help. Yet, is it his own power by which he helps and heals him? Ask him and he will tell you, no; it is but the carrying on of a power which took hold of *him;* and if you trace back all this sense of help, in man, you simply come through the long ages back to Paul's "I can do all things through Christ who strengtheneth me!"

So come the healing forces of God, pulsing along the ages, through the world,— working in the powers of Nature and the best thoughts and lives of men; not passing by even a poor crustacean that has lost its claw, or a tree that has been battered by the storm; but lavishing their subtlest care on the bruised bodies, and weak and ailing lives of men; and coming, in divinest ways of mercy and help, to sin-sick souls, and all the o'erwearied and unblessed, who lie about the byways of the world.

So has God led on the onward movement of His world, and leads it still. And we are to be His Helpers!

THE WORLD'S DEBT TO CHRIST

WHAT does the world really owe to Christ? In past time the answer was comparatively easy. Because, for one thing, Christ stood to men as God appearing in human form — something visible and tangible to look to and to pray to: and, for something almost more momentous, it was held that he had paid the penalty of the world's sin by a substituted sacrifice which was to be for ever the only escape of Man from Hell.

But this answer does not meet the real question as it is coming up at the present day. Even those who most cling to the divineness of Jesus, are growing less sure of his having been God in that visible, objective sense. And the atonement instead of being the old substituted sacrifice, is now put as the method of God's love for drawing His children towards Him. In fact Christ's work in the world is, more and more, coming to be regarded not as an isolated divine expedient to rescue mankind from a breakdown, but as a part of the divine education and development of the race.

Well, but what, then, has been Christ's part in this? Man, by God's mercy, has had many helpers. Why, then, from all the teachers and leaders who have passed across the page of history, single out Jesus for such peculiar and permanent reverence? That is the question for us. I put aside, indeed, all idea of his having been different from the rest of humanity by any superhuman birth. One of the most precious things in his wonderful life, is, its closeness to our own, not an instance of the Godhead coming down, but of humanity lifted up and evermore lifting us up. And so, indeed, I think the whole matter may be summed up in this: that the world owes to Jesus Christ the noblest, furthest reaching influence towards truth and goodness,— an influence which, first taking hold of his immediate followers and making them new men, went forth through them in ever widening circles to mankind, and still operates unspent to-day. That was what those first followers meant, in speaking of "the grace of the Lord Jesus Christ"— simply that nameless influence which they felt working in themselves and saw working in others. Very curious is the way in which that influence, took hold, and has kept hold ever since. My old tutor, John James Taylor — one of the most fair-minded students of history — used to say that even if all personal mention of Jesus had been lost, the changing aspect of history about his time, and the development of new feelings and thoughts in the world, would force us to conclude that some extraordinary influence must have been at work to produce it.

That influence can be traced working along two lines: in new convictions of Human Duty, and in a clearer and brighter sense of Divine Relations and Realities.

1. We owe to Christ, a new thought of Man — man's life, man's duties, man's relation to his fellow man. Man, as such, was cheap in the ancient world. There was a strange carelessness of human life. Suicide was no sin; hardly was infanticide. The sports of the great cities were murderous combats in which the lives of men were of no more account than the lives of beasts. Wherever Christianity came, life acquired a new sacredness; Suicide became a dreadful sin; Infanticide, as an institution, disappeared. Christianity had made the nobler heathens ashamed of their ferocious, sports before it had itself gained the power to suppress them. But, most of all, did this same reverence for man, as man, shew itself in the treatment of the poor, the weak, and especially of the sinful. Every form of Heathenism deified Strength, and

regarded the weak and incapable with contempt. I do not mean that there was not any kindness towards these in the old world, but that there was hardly any sense of duty to them,— and of a divine meaning in the very fact of the strong and the weak existing side by side. But wherever Christianity came, it set men caring for the sick, the crippled, the dying, and the degraded, — as an essential part of Christianity, and raised·up institutions of such care, I do not say absolutely new, but to an extent before utterly undreamed of.

It was this new Christian sense of the sacredness of man as man which led to the gradual abolition of slavery. I am not aware in all ancient history of a single sign of the feeling of slavery being wrong, or of any effort to do away with it. We have seen slavery defended in our own day, though only by the mischievous theory of the Old Testament being as divine and authoritative as the new. But, till Christ had come and gone, men were not even conscious of there being anything in slavery to defend. Certainly Paul advised Onesimus to go back to his former master; but he wrote with him to Philemon: "Receive him, not now as a slave, but as a brother beloved." Paul might not distinctly see it; but the religion which began by claiming for the slaves among its members the place of " brothers beloved " really sealed the fate of slavery.

The letter and the form, Churches and Priest-hoods, have, indeed, often enough been instru-ments of oppression; but the weak and the op-pressed have always felt, that the spirit of Christ was on their side. The strongest appeal of the mediæval satirists who lashed the worldliness and corruption of Christ's churches, was always to the simple loving life of Christ himself. And so, charity, at least, never failed, — and though that, too, often did harm — and sometimes does it still — yet it keeps rising to better and more thought-ful ways of helping. And there is one form of Christian charity, that, I think is almost abso-lutely new in Christianity, I mean the love and pity for the sinful and degraded, the longing to win them out of their lost state, the thousand-fold unceasing effort to save men and women back to goodness — I think that this is the crown-ing outcome of that sense of human worth and human brotherhood which Christ brought home to mankind, as a living and imperishable motive.

Again, the world owes to Christ the highest teachings and the strongest assurance of spirit-ual things. It is noticeable how these two have gone together in his work. He made religious

things the most spiritual that they have ever
been, the most entirely of the inward life, invisible, intangible; and yet none has ever made
men feel them so intensely real. And I am upon
very broad ground now — for even those who
in the present day most protest against keeping
the thought of Christ himself so prominent in
this spiritual religion, constantly refer to the high
pure Theism which they say Christ taught, only,
they think he meant us to hold that faith of his,
not to associate his name, and the memory of
him, with it. I think that is a question of which
way we can best realize that faith and keep hold
of it. But anyhow, whether we are to permanently associate our faith with him or not, it
is impossible to help feeling what a debt we owe
to him for it. Why, the whole field of religious
faith has been a new thing to men, since Christ
came. The thought of God has been a new thing.
Of course there have been many of the older
thoughts which have still lingered on, and often
alloyed and coarsened his pure Theistic teaching.
But at the heart of Christianity, the thought of
God has been a new thing, a holier, tenderer,
more loving presence,— differing from anything
that either Greeks or Jews had any real idea of
before. So also has Prayer. The thought of
Prayer, the feeling about prayer, which Christ

left among his disciples, and which, ever since, has given the key note to the piety of Christendom, was a new thing in the world. Prayer was much more of a formality before, a matter for priests to do, or a petition for certain definite gifts or help,— the lowly homage of subjects prostrate before a great King. You find hardly a trace before, — except here and there in the very loftiest of the Psalms — of that pouring out of the heart to God as to a friend, and of that joy in such personal communion, which sprang up at once in the early church, and which all through the Christian ages has given the peculiar character — so homelike and loving — to the piety of those who have really caught the spirit of Christ.

And, also, Immortality has been a new thing to men, since Christ's time. Of course I do not for a moment mean to claim Immortality as something of which mankind had no knowledge until Christ revealed it. The fact seems rather to be that as man's life, and consciousness of life, developes, at a certain stage belief in life to come is a part of man's development. So that, even if it be true that, in the very lowest grades or Savagism, tribes are found with no thought of a hereafter (though this is by no means certain) some thought of it is Universal wherever life has reached to the clear, full, human stage. And sometimes — as among the ancient Egyptians, this belief has become tremendously realistic — and so again among the Persians, from whom the Jews seem to have imbibed the thought, as a part of Religion, during the Captivity. But take the world as it was when Christianity came, and the belief in Immortality was a dim, distant shadowy thing, a joyless spectral state, only a degree better than annihilation. It seemed to have little moral relation to the present. It did not make the sinner more afraid of sin, nor the good man more strong in his righteousness. Especially in the Greek and Roman religions, it was like a faint shadow of the present, — as it has well been called, " an aftershine of the sun that had set, not a new day." Indeed it always seems to me one of the strongest tokens of how belief in life to come, is a very part of man and so must be true, that even so faint and joyless as it was, with nothing to lead man to love it, still the belief in it, in the people at large, never shewed any sign of dying out. But Christ made the hereafter a new thing to men — a real glorious world, a continuation of this present life, — this present life, not weakened and its vitality faded out, but strengthened and ennobled. Even the very exaggerations of his teachings, the extravagant realism of thrones, and crowns and harps, the strained literalizing of his parables of judgment into material hells and torments — even these arose from the new reality with which he invested the future life in man's thoughts. So it has been a new thing to men, ever since, more real, more living, more happy, something to rejoice in, and to think of with a tender, homelike trust, — such a feeling as Whittier expresses — that

> " Death is but a covered way,
> To lead us into life."

Of course, all this strong assurance of spiritual things which I thus trace to Jesus Christ, has weakened and deteriorated from what he left it. The Institutions, to which his influence gave rise have never been at all equal to the spirit and impulse which started them. But that is only human. The noblest movements, all along history, have always been belittled by those who have taken them up, and have been utilized and exploited for all manner of poor and selfish ends. But in watching the development of all the institutional life which grew out of Christ's influence, the striking thing is, really, not that the institution has been poorer than the originating

influence, but that the influence has still lived beyond the institution. Christ's influence, has, indeed, often seemed smothered and lost — but it
has risen up again; it has had not one resurrection but many resurrections. It has broken
out of its corruptions in uprisings of Reformation and the starting of new religious movements; and always the motive power of these
has been the spirit of the original Christ, as some
Huss or Luther, some Waldensian or Puritan,
a Fox or Wesley, a Channing or a Parker, has
caught the beauty and the power of it anew.
And this thing remains. It is not a mere historical memory, but a spirit that in strange and
subtle ways still takes hold of men and women
and " makes all things new." You can trace it
still to-day, in the common feeling of men quite
apart from ecclesiastical channels. You can
trace it in the very word " Christian." Just think
how that word is — not as defined by the
churches, but as felt — say by " the man in the
street " who very likely could not define it, and
has little faith in the way the churches would
define it! When common people see a good loving action, or a sweet self-sacrificing life — they
say, " Ah that's real Christianity!" So, even
those who openly denounce Christianity, as having a mischievous influence in the world, — if

they see a professing Christ doing some bad mean thing, are just as ready as any to attack his inconsistency and to cry " Where is your Christianity? " Thus, they unconsciously testify that in their deepest thought " Christianity " is a noble, beautiful thing, if you can only have it in its reality. And whence have they got that thought? from the traditional usage of the churches? No! The churches have, mostly, — all the ages through — protested against that use of the word " Christian," as designating the noblest, kindest goodness, — and have tried to limit it to some mere ecclesiastical meaning. But it has been too strong for them! Outside the churches, in man's common thought, and in the simple Gospels which constantly renew man's common thought, has come steadily down this large, kind, beautiful thought of duty and life which Christ taught — and lived — and it holds its place for ever. And that very thought, and the word which stands for it so vividly and pointedly, are part of the world's debt to him.

I know that it is often objected to all this that what I attribute to the influence of Christ is really partly due to the teachings and influence of other great lives before him, and partly to the general movement of civilization.

Well, by all means let us take all possible account of these causes, but I do not think they very much affect the value of what Christ has done for us. I rejoice in every great and wise word that in these days is being dug out from the sacred books of other religions. They find me a noble hymn from the Vedas; I delight in it; a fine saying of Confucius: thank God for that also; great sentences from Egyptian tombs; lofty sentiments from Greek Tragedians and philosophic Romans, parables and precepts from Hillel that are curiously like passages in the sermon on the mount. Good! But how do these things affect our debt to Christ? Archæologists find here and there some very good wheat in the mummy wrappings of Ancient Egypt. But it is not that on which we live. Those noble sayings of the ancient world have not much more to do with the real mental or moral condition of mankind, to-day, than that mummy wheat has to do with our bodily nourishment. They were great seed-thoughts, but for the most part they lay folded round with esoteric seclusion, or smothered in the embalm-ments of the dead past. As a matter of simple literary fact, it is Christianity itself, that has dug them out, or at any rate has brought them into the light of all this new appreciation of them! Why, it has been the Christian Missions in India which put Hindu Pundits

on the track of the pure original Theism which
really lay back of Brahminism; and it was even
European Sanskirt scholarship which shewed to
India that the text from the Vedas which was
always quoted as the authority for Suttee — the
burning of widows — had really no place in the
original Sanskrit. — No. What all this bringing out of the nobler religious thinking of the
ancient world has really done, is, to place the
whole subject of religion on a stronger foundation, — by shewing how all the best human
thought has always been tending in the same
direction; and so it has helped not to lessen but
to increase our debt to him, who carried it to
the highest point, and projected it with purer
and stronger power than ever before among the
enduring thoughts of the world. What those
thoughts could do, had been done. The ancient
world, was, in its higher culture, their work.
But it was not out of that culture that Christ
came. The ancient civilization was the very
thing that did not produce either Christ or Christianity, the very thing that most rejected and
opposed them. It is when I most realize the
grandeur of that ancient world, in its civilization,
its commerce, its literature, its art; it is when
I think of the magnificence of Rome and the
culture of Athens, and the Libraries and Col-

leges of Egypt — and, if you will, the learned Jewish schools of Jerusalem and Babylon, — it is then that I realize how feeble and fading was the best that they could do. And then I most feel what an immense debt we owe to that simple but majestic life which, growing up apart from all of these, gave men that living Word which was to survive through their decay, and to bring out what has well been called " A new Edition of human nature." Only one further question remains. Granting that Christ did all this in that far past when he lived and in the generations to which his personality was still comparatively near, is there anything to keep special hold of in the present?

I think there is.

I think the life-image which we have of Christ in the Gospels, is still the source of the very purest influence among men. I think the word and spirit of that life, are still a perpetually fresh revelation to the heart of moral and spiritual realities. Look where you will among all the struggle and service of mankind, from the slums of our great cities, to the villages of Pacific Islands, or the motley civilization of the East, — and — yes, there is plenty of that struggle and service, passing under the Christian name, which is as poor and clumsy as you will, — and, still, it is true that the very most earnest, and searching, and self-sacrificing working that is going on among men finds its best inspiration in the life and word of Jesus Christ.

And so I put it as the last element in this great debt of the world to Christ, that in him we have the noblest leadership of life. Life must have personal leadership or it will be apt to be all scattering, — scattering in its thought, scattering in its effort. I believe there is a profound truth in that parable of the vine and its branches. It is not more isolated living that we want, but growing, and acting, together, in loving brotherhood with the best life around us, and in loving communion of thought and following with all the best past life that has made us what we are; and all this long solidarity is closened to its strongest in earnest discipleship to the great Master of us all. It need not be any blind, unreasoning following — Christ, of all teachers, certainly never asked for that. With him, as always where the spirit of the Lord is, " there is Liberty " — but liberty is perfected not in self-conscious individualism, but in the loyalty of Love.

So, as I face the problems of this marvelous age; as I watch the workings of doubt; as I fol low the revelations of science which only lead us to a mystery they cannot penetrate; and as I note all the restless striving of the world for better life, — I am thankful for every light, and for all great teachers; — but, from them all, my heart turns back to Christ with something like that old cry of Peter's — "Lord to whom shall we go? Thou hast the words of eternal life!"

ANYTHING NEW IN CHRISTIANITY?

IT IS a question often asked in these investigating days. " How much in Christianity is new? " We all feel that it is — take it all in all — a mighty inspiration and uplifting of human life that has come to the world through Christ, but — how much was actually new? Not so much as used to be thought. It used to be thought that the whole of Christianity was a brand-new revelation, all before darkness and error. But as modern Scholarship has spelled its way into the ancient books of other religions, it has found there many a noble precept and truth once thought peculiar to the Bible; and, again, the study of evolution has shown that the religion of to-day has some of its roots away back of all history. And still, in that great onward movement of human religion which began in Christ, there was surely something new, and it is interesting to consider what it was.

Let us first give a thought to how much was not new. Why, almost the whole outward ap paratus and usages of Christianity were merely adaptations — and developments. The Church building itself was only a combination of the Jewish Synagogue and the Roman Basilica. The "Pontiff" was simply the "Pontifex," an old Roman title for the Pagan priest. The white surplice came from Egypt. The veneration for the Madonna was just the natural clinging to the Mother principle in Deity coming up in Christianity; and the very statues of the Virgin and child, were, to begin with, the old images of Isis with her infant Horus under a new name — as Pagan busts of Jupiter were sometimes made to do duty for St. Peter, and representations of Orpheus playing on his Lyre to the beasts, were adopted as types of Christ and his preaching. The Months of our year, and the days of our week bear traces of more than one old world Paganism, our Wednesdays and Thursdays, the days of Woden and Thor; January and March, the months of Janus and of Mars. "Easter" is simply the festival of the old Saxon Spring Goddess, "Eostre" changed to Christian uses. The fires of All hallows Eve are the old "Beltein," or Baal fires which probably came from Phoenicia and were lighted long before the time of Christ; and even Christmas itself, which we think our most peculiarly Christian festival, was not fixed upon from any real belief that Christ

was actually born then, but grew out of the almost world-wide festivals for the brightening
light and lengthening days after the winter
solstice, which seemed peculiarly appropriate
to associate with the coming of the great
light of Christ; and as for our Christmas cus-
toms, we get our mistletoe from the Druids, and
the Yule log from the Teutons, and our present-
giving from the Saturnalia of Ancient Rome.
Nay, to go into deeper things, even in what passes
for Christian doctrine, some has come from
quite other sources, and often it would have been
a great deal better if it had not! All that imagery of Hell. e. g. was not any special teaching
of Christ's. It was just the popular imagery
which has been in use for centuries. What Christ
made new about it was this: That while his
people said, " Those Hells are for the Gentiles "
— He said, " No! they are for the evil, the self
ish, the impure — Jews, just as much as Gentiles." Nay — the very doctrine of The Trin
ity, was not some new revelation of his about
God. It was only brought into Christianity long
afterwards, a mere distortion of the pure mono-
theism of Christ, derived directly from Neo-
platonism and back of that, from the old Poly-
theisms and triads of Greece and Egypt.

Even in the moral and spiritual realm, indeed,

something of the same kind is true. It is difficult
anywhere to draw any absolute line between what
Christ introduced and what men had thought
and felt before. One of the early English Free-
thinkers — Matthew Tindal — entitled his chief
work " Christianity as old as Creation " — and
the thought was a true one. The divine relations
and the human duties which the Gospel impresses
and lights up, were as old as creation. God
was as truly the Heavenly Father, men were
brothers, right was right, in the flint age, as to-
day. Yes, and not only these things were so,
but some men had glimpses of them. Long before Christ, great souls were groping their way
towards them. Here and there, in ancient religions, you come upon sayings and precepts
which are curiously like teachings of the Gospel. But what then? What is there, that is
wholly new? America had been discovered before Columbus, and steam before Watt. But that
does not lessen our debt to those who made
America an actual living place for men, and
steam an effective force. And so with what
Christianity has done for mankind. Even if
every one of its great moral and religious ideas
were in the world before — not the less is there a
wonderful newness in the place into which Christ
lifted them, and the power which he gave to them.

There is a passage in Dr. Martineau's "Ethics of Christendom" which brings out the broad outlines of this, so forcibly, that though it must be already familiar to many, I must venture to quote it: —

"Everyone is sensible of a change in the whole climate of thought and feeling, the moment he crosses any part of the boundary which divides Christian civilization from Heathendom. That (new) type is so strikingly original, its features so conspicuously express an order of passions and ideas strange alike to the Greek and Italian races, as to betray the creative action of some vast moral power, unborrowed from the established civilization." And he continues — "It seems an idle question for sceptical criticism to raise, whether the religion of Christ comprised in its teachings any element absolutely new. If genius had conceived it all before, life had not produced it until now; and the more you affirm the Philosophers' competency to think it, the more do you convict them of inability to realise it."

There is the general change which Christianity produced. But let us analyse it more closely. I think it is possible to distinguish some of the particular elements, both of Religion and of morals, which if not new, came out in a new char-

acter through Christ's influence and teaching.
Take for instance, the thoughts of God, and of
Prayer, and of Immortality. I know these were
not new with Christianity, but certainly in Christianity they take on quite a new tenderness and
nearness.

That teaching of God as the Heavenly Father;
— Certainly God had been called " Father " before Christ's time. It is beautiful to find that the
very first word for God among our old Aryan
forefathers in Central Asia, as we spell out their
thought in the old Vedic hymns, was " Dyaus-
Pithar " — Heaven-Father, and this reappears in
the " Zeus-Pater " of the Greeks, and the " Ju
piter " of the Romans. And this stood, undoubt
edly, for a thought of mighty beneficent sover-
eignty over the world — but it did not stand for
that close, tender, personal relation in which,
through the Christian centuries, people have
loved that word of Christ " Father in Heaven."
It might be the germ of that, but it was not
that. " Heavenly Father " as Christ said it, and
as every little child may learn to say it, and feel
it, now, is something new, something different
from anything that men felt before.

So again of communion between God and man.
I do not claim that the term " Holy Spirit "
stands for something absolutely new. Men had

prayed before, and every religion had believed
in some form of divine inspiration. But they
had believed in such divine guidance and help for
a few exceptional souls, specially favoured ones.
Nowhere comes out as in Christianity the faith
in the Spirit of God as an influence open to all.
And Christianity teaches it as so tender an influence! Perhaps the nearest to what Paul felt
as being " led by the spirit " and " constrained
by the spirit " to say this, or to do that, is what
Socrates felt — that inner light which he speaks
of as his " Daemon " — or " Guardian Spirit ";
but the " Daemon " of Socrates was a purely intellectual guidance, while the Holy Spirit is the
helper to moral strength, and especially " The
comforter." I hardly think that in the whole
range of religion, outside Christianity, you could
find such an expression as that " Grieve not the
Holy Spirit of God." And so in the humbler
ranges of Communion with God. Prayer has
been a new thing to the human heart since Christ
came; something nearer and tenderer; less of
the humble petition to an almighty king, more
of the happy confidence of the little child talking
to a Father or Mother.

So, of Immortality; of course it was not a new
belief, and yet it certainly began at once to take,
among the early Christians, a very different

place from what it ever seems to have done before. Before, it had practically been an exceptional glorification for sages or heroes; for all
else, a far off, faint, shadowy, washed out life,
nothing like as real and substantial as the life of
earth. But, at once in Christianity, you see an
entirely new feeling about it. It is a happy
home-like world, close upon this present; a life
— not faded or shadowy, but like the present life
only glorified, and more intensely real. And,
from that time, to all the best Christian life,
the thought of the Heavenly world has been that
of something very close and dear and beautiful.

Turn now to the Moral side of Christianity,
and you find the same thing. Of course its car-
dinal moral ideas were none of them absolutely
new. Three hundred years before Christ, Aris-
totle had written: — " In all times men have
praised honesty, moral purity and beneficence.
In all times they have protested against murder, adultery, perjury, and all kinds of vice."
And yet there was something new. The moral
life which was developed in the early Chris-
tion communities, the moral life which you
find struggling upwards through the Christian ages, is something different from what was
in the world before. It is at once intenser, and
more inspiring — and I think, more brotherly

and loving. Take the sense of sin for example. You find before Christianity, in the Greek Tragedies, e.g., terrible remorse for great crimes, — but that sorrowful sense of sinfulness in the presence of the pure holiness of God — that which has been intensely characteristic of the more earnest side of Christian life — that is a new thing! And that sense of Duty as an infinite self-consecration, that longing and striving for perfectness; — the best life of the Christian ages, has, as Martineau puts it, been " one long sigh after an unattained perfection " — I do not say that amounts to a great element, but it is certainly a new element in the religion of mankind.

Similarly it is, with brotherhood and mutual kindness and helpfulness, in Christianity. There was something of brotherhood before, but it has been wider and tenderer, since. " Philanthropy " is not an original Christian word, but in its larger sense, it is an original Christian thing. In the old world, it merely meant personal, private kindness or courtesy — and of that there was plenty in the world before Christ, but " Philanthropy " as a large clear duty of man to care for his brother man — " Philanthropy " as one of the wide spread efforts of organised society, that is a new thing. Of course, Christianity has not changed the world to its higher, wider thought of brotherliness. There has continued to be plenty of pride, plenty of caste-feeling, plenty of oppression, and a great deal even of actual slavery. That is only the common ground of human history. The new thing, is, that ever since Christ came, the thought and spirit with which he somehow touched men, has protested against all this, has kept striving to modify it, has kept up a standing effort, never entirely given up, even in the darkest ages always breaking out again — a standing effort after the truer, kindlier relation of human beings, which Chris tianity had taught.

And finally there is one direction which this higher human brotherliness has taken, which I think is entirely new with Christ and Christian ity. I mean the special anxiety for the sinful; and the loving, patient endeavour to save them from the sad, lost state of sin. The old Greek poet got so far as to say — "No man is a stranger to me provided he is a good man." Christ first taught men to feel that the bad man also is a brother, the lost woman a sister, to be sought, and loved, and helped back. Many of the great ancients got so far as to say that a magnani mous soul should forgive one who injures him; Christ teaches that we should try to do him good!

Possibly you may find a thought like this here and there in the older world, but Christ has made this a large, effective part of the organised life of Christendom. Of course in this too, our actual lags far away behind the ideal. We cannot look on the state of thousands in our great cities, without feeling sad, it is so little that we seem to do, to rescue them and make them better. True! But it is something that Christianity makes us sad for this; that it makes us feel that it is our concern; that it so makes men feel this, as to shape the doings of society, to make new issues of helpfulness in legislation, and to introduce new reformative elements into the administration of justice; and that thus, age after age, it keeps the most earnest life of Christendom to this distinctly new effort to save the world, and to save the lowliest soul in it, from sin.

There, then, is what Christianity has contributed of new to the higher life of mankind. You see, I have not made any extravagant claim — and yet, when you consider it, what a gain it is. For it is — a clear advance along the whole line both of divine relations and human relations. On the old fundamental religious thoughts — of God, and Prayer, and Immortality, a new light of close tender, happy, homelike feeling; along the

line of human Duty and Morality, a new as-
piration and restless striving after goodness; a
wider, more inclusive brotherhood; and this one
entirely new element, of anxiety to draw the
lost and sinful back into the happy family of
God.

I know that I have been speaking all through
more of what Christ has put into man's thought,
than of anything that has yet got built up into
Man's organic, social living.   So be it.   But it
is thought which in the end rules the world.
Christianity is still, much of it, only a prophecy,
— but it is a prophecy which ever holds to its
aims the best minds and hearts; and instead of
feeling, as some do, that we have about come
to the end of it, I feel more and more that we
are still only at the beginning of its onward way,
and only at the beginning also, of its marvellous
influences that help mankind along that onward
way.   Perhaps it seems pretty far along in history to talk of Christianity as only at its beginning.   And yet what else is it with all the development of man?   Only along the thousands of
years do we see any sign of steady gain.   It is
everything to find some living spirit and influence for onward higher life.   And that we have,
in Christ: and so the true thing is, to hold to that
living influence and to all that keeps it most liv-

ing in our hearts and among men — and even though it seems as yet to have brought us no further than what, in the light of the highest, are still but beginning; still, we must hold to it, and keep the closest to it that we can, and trust that, somehow, God is leading on the world, to His own perfect end.

ALL THINGS — BEGINNINGS

THE spirit of Christianity is that of a dim, but confident onlook to great possibilities for this poor human nature of ours. " Beloved, now are we the sons of God. And it doth not yet appear what we shall be." In a word, we are merely at the beginnings, yet even so are the objects of a divine love and care, children of God, inheritors of the promises, with vague glory-flashes of Prophecy always lighting up the future.

It is that subject, — Beginnings — that I want to dwell upon. The more I think of it, the more it seems to open out to larger and larger meanings, touching not man alone, but all the mighty world, until its has come to seem one of the great explanatory words which unlock the meaning of the world and life, that, after all, we are only at the beginning of things. And it is a thought which has seemed to whisper patience and courage in the midst of the perplexity and confusion of the world. For, look at things for what

they now are and there is plenty of discord, sometimes things which might almost drive us to
despair — things that shock and horrify us, and
set one asking " can God be good and such things
be?" And I do not say it makes all clear to
say — " Beginnings, things are only in their beginnings," but it makes it a little easier to believe that things may be working right, after
all, and so, easier to watch and wait, and still to
cleave to faith, amid whatever darkness there may
be.

And I think two things help us to this thought
of all things being only beginnings: one, from
science, the observation of outward nature; the
other from religion, taking that as summing up
the suggestions and intuitions which come to
us from our inward nature. Outward Nature
shews us a vast past — ever vaster — of Evolution, slow developments, from beginnings which
look chaotic, to gradually higher forms first of
organism, then of life. Then as soon as we have
come to man, a new process begins, and his instincts or intuitions, what you will, take up
man's thinking, his dim feeling of something beyond, towards a limitless future. And the great
progressive meaning of the first process, seems
to give us the master thought of the whole. Because, the world is not an incoherent world, all

in confusion. From the first grouping of its atoms, order is everywhere. And with such perfect order at the basis of things, can we think of less order in their outcome. So we are brought to man, and what his life and being are coming to. It seems to have been the crown of all that long unfolding, when man's rude consciousness of Being, leaped up into the further consciousness of more life to come. At first it might be only of some future of retribution, and that, widening out into the idea of the better life going on to perfection; but as you take in the significance indeed of life to come, there is no stopping in it, anywhere; and so it has led men on — not all men perhaps, but the highest thinkers — on and on — gradually brushing aside all halting theories of finalities, last days, grand windings up of providence and judgment, — until we are brought to such sense as I am trying to shape out, of how we are still only as it were at the beginning of things — and all things, beginnings.

Let me just remind you, in passing, that this thought of vast futures and possibilities of Progress does not in any way weaken the moral force of the other thought of retribution. That idea of the moral sequences of life, is true — one of the deep fundamental laws of being, —

"Our past still travels with us from afar
"And what we have been, makes us what we are."

Yes, that is part of God's great truth, and part
which does not wait for the great " judgment "
— or, truer, as Paul calls it " Revelation of Judgment," in going on into the life beyond.   Each
day, here, is partly a judgment on yesterday;
this year or last year.   Manhood is partly a judgment on youth; old age, is partly a judgment
on full life.   And so the future life is a judgment
on this.   But still — surely it is not judgment
only.   In all these successions of life, the
future brings not only something of judgment
on the past, but also something of new impulse, and new opportunity.   There comes in
one of the openings of further truth that Christ
did not enter upon, hardly more than hinted at
— the ultimate possibilities of poor, sinful, un-
developed life, in the Infinite future — But he
left it lying not in darkness, but in the great
enfolding light of a Father's love, and it is in
the light of that love that it is so helpful to look
on, remembering that all things are beginnings.
But while this thought does not really lessen that great truth of moral retribution on which
Christianity laid such stress, what a new light of
hope and emphasis it throws on so much of the

onward looking of human Philosophy and Religion. " The world is a becoming " said Heraclitus. It is often hard to believe — the movement seems, in many parts of the world, so slow! Yet in the larger stir and movement of mankind the trend is unmistakeable. The good, the wise are not mere incidents but prophecies. The Bible pages glow with words of splendid faith in some greater destiny for man. All higher approach to God, seemed promises of what all might become. " Would that all the Lord's people were prophets! " cried Moses — and Joel said that in the last days, they should be. The very note of all Christ's gospel was that all were children of the Infinite Father! And the VIII. chapter of Romans, — the greatest chapter of Paul's greatest epistle — is all alive and glowing with the thought of a Creation struggling upwards, all the world's groaning and seemingly chaotic evil, simply the travailing of Nature for the new birth of a redeemed humanity. And so comes in that key-word of John's, " Now are we the children of God," he says, now, even now, in this poor, weak, sinful, stage of us — " and it doth not yet appear what we shall be," only in that greater life in which Christ was and the saints, we, too, " should be like him," the perfectest thing that they could think of. It is these great thoughts, which have gradually worked upon the hearts of Christian thinkers, quenched all narrow dogmas of election, made the idea of any being finally "lost," more and more impossible in the universe of a God of love, and set the key-note of the gospel of Universal hope: and it is this thought which, the more we follow it out, means, that all this life now and here, is mere beginning.

"All things beginnings." I think it throws a larger light on Nature, and larger still upon human nature, on all the great human world. Why, even in the very knowledge of our time — this wonderful science, — it is constantly forced upon us that with all the progress men have made, we are still only at the begin ning. We are just getting glimpses even in this very time, of facts and forces, and a whole realm of wonder, utterly undreamed of as late as when we elders were children. We have passed behind the visible and the tangible, into a world within the world. We are hardly more than peeping into it here and there, at a few points, — in these "x" Rays; and this electricity that passes silently through earth or stone as readily as along our wires — and all the mysteries of Biology — but what a wonder realm it all is, and even these things are but "beginnings," and I think the whole touches our hearts with a new awe, as well as wonder. But it is not in the qualities and possibilities of the material universe that this thought seems to come most strikingly, but in thinking of the qualities of the life in man. I think of it in regard to friendship and love. " The most wonderful thing in the world " Henry Drummond called love. And here and there men always have had glimpses of what it might be. Even in what we call friendship how it enriches life. You love your friend so that you would gladly tread the paths of life very near to one another — fight its battle as comrades, take closest counsel of its great thoughts, work out its problems together — and lo! the friction of fortune and the compulsion of imperious necessities drift you apart; and one of you may have to toil along in a London counting house, and the other brings up in some lonely up-country station in India — and all the years apart you never meet another friend you care for as much; and you exchange letters now and then — but what is that as any fulfilment of " Friendship "? And once in many years perhaps, you meet, and you talk of the old times, and it seems so good to be together — but then again the strokes of life beat out the hour of parting — and the express moves out, or the ship sails away —— Is that the

world's final thing in friendship? Rather, a
wonderful glimpse of what might be one of the
most blessed things in life: — but we only just
touch the beginnings of it!

Or take that closer, intenser friendship we
specially call love — so constantly " beginning,"
hardly a life without some beginning some time
of it — but so often coming to nothing, and so
often draggling down into mere, commonplace
living together, or degraded by the sway of poor,
base passions; or getting into inextricable tangle
with the very institutions which itself has caused;
and even when it does seem as if it came to its
purest and its best — something that should last
for ever — then, by and by — the inevitable parting! — and, what beyond? Ah! who shall solve
the meaning of all this? I know not; — but it
comforts me to hear this thought whispering itself to me — " We are but at the beginnings of
things! " I know not how it may all be — but a
thought comes, in such a word as Emerson's: —

> " What is excellent,
> " As God lives is permanent."

And so it is again, — constantly the same kind
of perplexity, but ever the same refuge, in all
the moral tangle and incompleteness of the world.
Even in the very elements of moral life at all, the

perplexity haunts us. Why, what is " sin "? We seem, at times, to have some clear knowledge of it. We repeat the commandments, noting how in the main essentials, they are so alike among all peoples; and yet what is it makes the wrong thing wrong, and makes it wrong to do it however much it gives us some great pleasure, or seems to offer relief from some great palpable trouble? We cannot tell, or at least it is very easy to confuse ourselves even when the telling has seemed clearest! and so the world is full of palpable vices, and overwhelming wrongs, and horrors that seem rather reversions to the Ape and Tiger, than to come in any line of progress we can trace. And even where we seem to trace a little progress, what does it amount to? Here in this civilized England what is it we have really attained? Mere hints of better things to come — always with an underside of seething want and misery and passionate revolt against the present order of things, which touch one with the sense of how poor and unsatisfying it all is. Yes, and yet all through, and in and out among these confused and fragmentary rights and wrongs, that curious sense of right, that longing for a better nobler world, that irrepressible striving for it, that reverence for those who in spite of temptation keep the line of Duty.

As I walk amidst it all, it still keeps coming
to me, — " Beginnings! we are only at the beginnings," we are only at the beginning of this
nature of ours, only at the beginning of this
human society, for which our very Nature com-
pels us to strive, but from which the best that we
can compass seems so far! Only at the begin
ning of ourselves! God help us if it were not
so, if the better thoughts which in bright mo-
ments, lift us up to such high " mounts of vision "
such consciousness of what Life might be — God
help us indeed if the significance of such better times is measured by our weakness and selfishness, and depths of conscious evil into which
we sink at times. But then, too, comes this
thought — We are only at the beginning!

What is the upshot of it all? Any clear doctrine taught, any exact truth that science or
Theology can catalogue among its facts or
truths? No; nothing so certain and defined as
that. But it does seem to me a thought which
widens out our Theologies and all the thoughts
which men have shaped into their doctrines of
last things, into larger meanings of Divine Love
and endless possibilities of hope. It helps me to
look upon the world, and on every poorest life in
it, with a little less heart-sinking as for hopeless failure. I see an idiot child; I hear the

cursing of some foul-mouthed human brute; I see the poor, bent old woman whose very looks tells of a stunted life of coarse and sordid toil; I read the sad statistics of pauperism and crime — and all the degradation that haunts the night-side of our cities — I read the story, day by day, of all the warring, suffering, sinning world — and I do not think it makes one feel the sadness of it less, or makes one less anxious to do anything to help it wherever one can reach with any touch of healing, but ever the thought comes in : — " Beginnings ; — only beginnings " and I feel a little less dismay — a little more trustful and hopeful of some ultimate good. I feel more sure that silently, through what at times seems such confusion, — an order is working, and a Providence of goodness, and a supreme and infinite Wisdom.

THE VEILED LIFE IN MAN

PAUL's famous saying "Now we see thro' a glass darkly but then, face to face; now I know in part, but then shall I know even as also I am known" is commonly quoted as a saying about religious things, — of how we see such great realities as God and eternity only as through a glass darkly. And it is deeply true that way, but that was not what Paul was speaking of. He was speaking of Man and how Man is only darkly seen — and of the hidden good in man. The whole chapter is about "charity." "Love" the revised version renders it; and love is the commonest translation of Paul's word, and yet I like "charity" better here for it is that large impersonal kind of love, which Paul is speaking of — and "charity" seems to express that better — that which "hopeth all things" and "believeth all things" — not just of those we love. And this is his closing thought about such "charity" — that if we will have faith for it here, if we will keep on loving our fellow-creatures even when we cannot see much in them worth loving — our faith shall there be justified; for here we only see each other through a glass darkly, but there face to face — and there — looking " face to face," " knowing even as we are known " we shall find not less good than we thought, but more good than earthly charity ever hoped.

What a searching thought of the Hereafter — that seeing " face to face " — and yet he seems to have felt it a large hopeful thought too. And Paul was no easy-going optimist. He saw with terrible clearness the sinful side of human nature; it lay right about him in those old Heathen cities with a frightful plainness; and yet even Paul with his clear sight of it, is not dismayed. Over it all, he sees the Love of God, and through it all he sees something better in man, and so he puts it that there, where all is known, there where we shall judge not with these poor childlike judgments of earth — there will be more to love than to hate.

But the larger, general thought comes first — the thought of what a veiled hidden life this is altogether in man — only half seen; — it may be a thought of charity and hope — in the end of all it is; but it is a thought with a great deal more in it than that — a great deal of searching, and awfulness, and even dread, before we get to the hope and the charity.

We know how it is, when we think about it. Here in this life we do see each other only " as through a glass darkly." The word was even more forcible in Paul's day, for they had only poor, clouded glass, or talc to see through — which, like our frosted glass, only showed the vaguest image of the person behind it. And is not that about how we see people? The flesh acts as a veil to the spirit. Pass along the street. Look in the faces of those whom you meet. How many of them can you read at all? There you see one whose face repels you — telling some unmistakable story of self-indulgence, avarice or cruelty, and yet perhaps only half telling it! There, again, is one whom at a glance we feel we should like to know — a face with the lines of high-thought on it, or the look of goodness, or an earnest capable manhood born of struggle and endeavour. Yet even with these you only get the faintest outline of the life within, and with the vast majority of faces you do not get even that. And yet every one of the thousands whom you meet has an inner life — an inner life like no one else's — an inner life story, stranger than any fiction if it should be truly told.

Nay, it is so even with those whom you think

you know. Do you know them? There are some perhaps with whom the ordinary disguises of the world are laid aside. You know them, and they you — thoroughly! And yet is it so? You go a good way in, in that intimacy, but not to the innermost. You talk of very deep experiences — but even those dressed up a little — and not of the very deepest. You confess your weaknesses—do you ever tell all? Hardly! There is an innermost self knowledge into which no other may come. Does a man ever tell how near he has sometimes come to black ugly sins that no one dreams of suspecting — or perhaps how he has passed the line — done something that can never be undone through all eternity? From this side of our now seeing and being seen only "as through a glass darkly" pass on to that "face to face" It is not Paul's thought alone! It is part of the very instinct which sets man looking on to further life, that there we shall all be seen as we are! All the great interpreters of that silent word of God which shapes itself through man's holiest thoughts — all teach this, that all this mask and disguise is only of the present and the outward and the earth. There we pass out of the twilight into the open day. There every soul must appear not as it wishes to be, not as on earth it has tried to appear, and perhaps succeeded in appearing, but as it is! Well might Christ say — " Many that are first shall be last!"

This is a thought of awe — this of our lives lying open to the gaze of others. But I do not know if it is not almost more awful still to think how we shall see ourselves, there, with perfect truth. Perhaps the most terrible power of deception we possess, is that of deluding ourselves. Carlyle says that the worst kind of cant is that of people who have talked cant till they have come to believe in it and to feel a sort of sincerity in it. So people sometimes talk about religion and busy themselves over its forms and observances and the externalities of Religion, till they come to fancy themselves really religious! So a man may give, right and left, and feed upon the cheap praise of his generosity until he verily believes himself a really benevolent character. Yet shall we throw stones at these? Don't we all delude ourselves to some extent in the same fashion? Don't we salve over the ugly spots, and magnify the little good things we have to show? Yes! We do it now — but it will be impossible, then! I think that is one of the most awful thoughts of the life to come, more awful — when you really face it — than any images of outward fire

or pain? Do you remember how the thought
is worked out in that little poem of one sitting
" alone with conscience "?

> I sat alone with my conscience
> In a place where time had ceased,
> And we talked of my former living
> In the land where the years increased.
> And I felt I should have to answer
> The question it put to me,—
> And to face the answer, and question,—
> Through all eternity.
>
> The ghosts of forgotten actions
> Came floating before my sight,
> And things that I thought were dead things
> Were alive with a terrible might;
> And the vision of all my past life
> Was an awful thing to face—
> Alone with my conscience sitting
> In that solemnly silent place.
>
> *   *   *   *
>
> And I thought of my former thinking
> Of the judgment day to be;
> But sitting alone with my conscience
> Seemed judgment enough for me!
>
> *   *   *   *
>
> And I felt that the future was present,
> And the present would never go by,
> For it was but the thought of my past life
> Grown into eternity.

Then I woke from my timely dreaming
And the vision passed away;
And I knew that the far-away warning
Was a warning for to-day.
  *   *   *   *
And so I sit, now, with my conscience
In the place where the years increase,
And I try to remember the future
And I know—of the future judgment—
How dreadful so e'er it be,
That to sit alone with my conscience,
Will be judgment enough for me!

Ah! And yet, by God's mercy, not that **for** ever! One can hardly think that an eternity of remorseful looking back is the best thing that God has in store, even for his sinfullest children. Still — that is in it, — whatever ultimate hope opens out beyond it, and if it is an awful thought, it is also a wholesome one. If there is anything in you that you would dread to have known, and dread to face, even by yourself — clear it away, now. Yes, even though it be like cutting off a hand or plucking out an eye. Yes, even though clearing it away mean some open change, and confession and shame, — that was a deep word of Mohammed's — " Better to blush in this world than in the world to come " !

It was not, however, for these thoughts of warning that Paul spoke of the inner life being

seen " face to face " in the life to come and no
longer " through a glass darkly." He spoke of
it, especially, for its meaning of love and hope.
If there is worse in men than those about them
know — perhaps than they even know themselves
— what is specially in his mind is that there
is better, too. It is a word of the Infinite, patient, divine Love, and of how our love should
be as like it as we can — and of how, in the end
of all, that love, whether divine or human, that
has clung to the good in men, shall be justified.
Sometimes we hardly feel as if it could be so.
We see people who appear to us so mean, so bad,
so lost to every nobler feeling — that it seems
impossible to think of love for them. And when
we scorn ourselves, as all honest souls have to do
at times — for some hidden baseness — we feel
as if — should that be unveiled — all would
scorn. And yet, even in that very self-scorn, if
we have learned at all Christ's thought of the
Heavenly Father, we know God does not scorn
us. I do not mean that we learn any thought of
His being merely what some one has called " a
good natured God." It is rather the sense of
an Infinite divine Patience — a love which never
seems to change or tire — which even in its
sharpest discipline is trying to do us good, and
which will have us saved — will never leave us to

have peace in any wrong or sin. I think that is the love which Christ touches in his own love for the poor, weak lives about him. Even when his words seem to us most scathing, it does not follow that they sounded so as he spoke them. Some one objected once in talking to Dr. Channing, to Christ's denunciations of Woe to the Pharisees; they were so harsh and fierce he said. Dr. Channing took up the Testament and read them—that terrible rebuke with its ever-recurring refrain — " Woe unto you Pharisees ! " — and he read them, in the light of his own feeling of the dignity of Man and of the infinite sorrow that it is when man sinks all away from it. " Ah," said the objector " if Christ spoke like that, of course I could not say anything." But was not that just how he did speak ! And so in that deep word of St. John's — "Even if our heart condemns us, God is greater than our heart and knoweth all things "! And as with God so with those who see with the cleared sight of His heavenly world. — As Tennyson says —

> " Ye watch, like God, the rolling hours
> With larger, other eyes than ours,
> To make allowance for us all."

And Father Faber's beautiful word comes in —

" There is no place where earth's sorrows
   Are so felt as up in Heaven:
There is no place where earth's failings
   Have such kindly judgment given."

Why, our own poor lives in their best hours
might teach us something of this. We feel what
it is, at times, to have the thought of God's will
and to long with unutterable longing for higher
and better things; — and yet, we have to live
out our lot in the throng of the world's tempta-
tions and to fight down our passions, and to
bear up against the wear and tear and burden of
life! What a struggle! Why, I fancy that even
the strongest seldom feels that he comes to any
victory. And what must it be then to the weak, to
those who come into the world with taint of temptation in their very blood — or with some great
overmastering passion in them — as so many
do. Or, what must the struggle be to those who
have that curious lack you often see of any force-
ful will, or to those who from childhood are
trained in mean and frivolous and selfish ways.
God be patient with us all, and help us to be
patient with each other! We want more tolerance. It is not an easy world, this, even for the
strong — but what is it for the weak? This
is no world for the weak, at least not if there
is no mercy or help but man's. For the world

is hard on the weak, soon tires of helping them, soon gives them up. Is it not because we see " only through a glass darkly " ?

> " What's done we partly may compute
> But know not what's resisted."

— If we knew all, many a harsh word would be checked. And so that saying of how here we see each other only through a glass darkly is a word not only of hope for the life beyond, but of more patient tolerance and helpfulness and kindness here in this life. We are only at the beginning of things here. That is the key to all the moral tangle of the world. Only at the beginning of things, — not only in the poor savage life that seems in some aspects of it, to have developed here not very much above the brutes — but also in the criminal life that seems sometimes in its awful depths of vice and animalism to mock at our theories of human progress. The hidden good seems so far down, so hard to come at — that, in our short time view, we fall to wondering if it is there at all, if there is anything really human to lay hold of, and to afford the moral leverage towards any nobler being. Talk as if all was settled here — just one brief probation of this 60 or 70 years — and then all saved, or, all lost. As well might the angels

have looked down on the age of the great Sau-
rians and watched

> "The monsters of the prime
> That tare each other in their slime."

— and thought that was the end, and wondered
what it meant. Still — in this higher range of
man's being, we are only at the beginnings;
though, thank God, even in the beginnings we see
such flashings up of a nobler humanity, and
even where all seems worst and most hopeless,
such unexpected traits of some thing good as
prophecy to us what may be in the illimitable
future. It is a veiled, half crippled, half developed life we achieve at the best, a life with a
strange mystery both about its evil and its good
— " all, but half seen and darkly " — but yet a
life haunted with the sense of better things than
ever we attain. It is only " through a glass
darkly " that we see any of it — only dimly discerning our real selves, only partially knowing
others, only getting fleeting glimpses of the
things which yet at times, we know are the
everlasting realities of Being. And so, again I
thank God for these great words, which, here and
there, in the inspired hours of loftiest souls, rise
above these poor beginnings, see visions of an
Infinite wisdom and goodness working slowly

towards diviner things and tell us that in the
end the darkness shall be changed to light and
love and hope be justified. All the struggle of
heart, and conscience by which in our short
earthly span we ourselves seem to make so little
way; all the patient love for weak and way-
ward ones about us, which here seems so often
vain; all the long toil and battle for making the
world a better, cleaner world, which here seems
to bring so little victory — there, in the light,
these shall be made plain. There we shall understand better the fulness of that Divine Love,
which here we fall to questioning because our
own love seems to fall so short of any effect.
And so the Faith, the hope, the trust in some
wiser power than ours, to which we cling as
we grope our way through the moral mystery of
the world, shall there abide, prove to be the real
everlasting reality. That is Paul's meaning. It
is the word of an absolute confidence in love and
hope for man, which shall be justified hereafter,
however little they seem to come to here! Here
we see only " through a glass darkly "; and yet
even here, we catch glimpses of the truth in
Nature, an outward trend of beneficial meaning, in the changes of the earth, and the perishing and developing types of star and plant and
beast. Is it less sure in Man, a hidden good

which is God's very meaning in His creatures, and which in all struggling, sinning, repenting, praying lives of Men, is groaning and travailing for something greater than we can see? And so abideth " Faith " in this hidden good in man — and " hope " for it to conquer in the end — but greatest of all is " love " that still, through all, keeps loving, and pitying, and striving and praying for the good, and never faileth — and knows that somehow God shall justify it at last.

THE MYSTERY OF GOODNESS

THE greatest mystery of the Universe is the mystery of Goodness.

Not the mystery of Evil or Sin. It is in regard to these that the world has put the stress of its wonder, in the modern questioning of the problem of Being. God has been taken for granted; but how in the world did sin and evil come? So the true order has been reversed throughout. We hear of "the mystery of pain," but we seldom hear such a phrase as "the mystery of happiness." So the world of thinkers has been occupied with grave discussions about the origin of evil, and the mystery of sin. But hardly ever is such a subject mooted as, "the mystery of Goodness."

And yet it was directly suggested in the old Scriptures. "Great is the mystery of godliness," wrote Paul and it was only the perversity of theological textualism which switched off the attention of Christendom from the magnificent thought of the grandest quality in Creation manifested to us in Christ to a doctrinal dispute as to whether the exact method of that highest manifestation involved an assertion that Christ was God.

To that grandest quality we go back, as the deepest mystery in the economy of the Universe. Godliness is a great word in the New Testament and always in the same meaning of the higher kind of human goodness, — goodness not of any mere conventional legal morality kind, but goodness rooted in God, and looking up to God.

And now does any one ask, Where is the special helpfulness of emphasizing that the great mystery of Being is in this Godliness, this higher kind of goodness? Perhaps I can indicate it best by telling how the help of it actually came to me. It was in talking with a friend who had come to me sorely oppressed and troubled with the sense of all the wickedness which there is, the dreadful crimes that darken the story of the world from day to day, the deep viciousness which we constantly see, and which sometimes seems almost irredeemable, — yes, and the sense of how there is so much of it in ourselves, so that often those who perhaps seem outwardly good feel in their own souls dreadful possibilities of sin which at times crush them almost into despair. " Oh! " my friend said, and he spoke wth an agony of spirit that I can never forget: " How does it

come? What does it all mean? Why is it that
there is all this sin in the world and in our
selves? Why is it that we do such mean, bad
things? Why is it that, even after we have been
praying, and feeling as if we could never do
wrong any more, we so often go and forget the
good, and do the very opposite?" "Till," he
said, "sometimes it sets me wondering whether
it is any use, — and this praying and trying and
struggling, — whether one might not as well
let all go."

And then it was that there flashed into my
mind this thought I am putting to you here; and
I said: "O, my friend, I feel all this just as
you do; and I do not know that I can help you
much. Only, are not we looking at it all, for one
thing, in the wrong way, from the wrong end,
as it were? We are talking as if all this evil
in us and in the world were wonderful, such a
mystery! Is it not really the good that is the
mystery? This haunting good, that rebukes the
bad in us, however natural and tempting the bad
may seem, — how does *this* come? — this good
that will not let us rest in sin, however much
we want to do; that makes us ashamed of it,
and long to be free from it, and that no sin or
evil seems utterly to crush out of us, or out of the
world, and that age after age has kept lifting

mankind a little higher, and that still keeps up **the** struggle, though it often does seem to accomplish so little?

The more I have thought of all this since, the more I have felt that this is the true way of looking at the matter, and that it makes it, at any rate, not quite so dark and hopeless. Of course, I do not mean to say that this is the whole account of the mystery of our moral being, that it is all solved by putting the stress of our wonder, not upon how evil came to be, but upon how good comes and goodness and all the sense of goodness and the striving for it. Of course, it is just as great a mystery, if we talk of beginnings, how came anything to be? How came matter? Still more, how came life? But human knowledge has pretty well accepted the fact that these are not to be known, simply to be accepted. Science begins with what is, — a world, and life in it, and, evidently, as far back as we can trace, the struggle for existence, everything striving to be and to continue to be, a teeming, seething world of life, with everything writhing and scratching and clawing in the struggle for its place and its food, and for the continuance of its being. And all this has come to seem, in a fashion, natural. Granted a world of life and living things, and selfishness and struggle for self seem as if they might originate themselves. The tiniest animalcule can be conceived of, and can hardly be conceived of as other than climbing upward, over everything in its way, and struggling, with a dumb, unconscious force, to make good its own footing in the world in which it finds itself. And, out of such struggling, warring life, one can also understand, in a fashion, the stronger surviving, and such stronger life adapting itself to the world's conditions by slow, wonderful changes, and the struggle growing continually more complicated and far-reaching. Granted all that, and there is no particular mystery in all that we call evil. Indifference to others, greed, lust, — they would not be evil in such a beginning of the world, but just its natural forms and forces working themselves out. And, if you can imagine such clash of forces killing out all but the strongest or cunningest, and gradually working up through brute-life to man, — still, what savagism, to begin with! And, if the whole thing be only what man (beginning in that savagism, or beginning further back still among the brutes) has made of himself, nothing specially wonderful or mysterious in much of that savagism lingering on, or in constant reversions to it! As you see what that original struggle for self is still in its lower ani-

mal forms, I do not think we need much explaining how all that we call " evil " comes still
to be, — all forms of lust and cruelty and self-
indulgence, even such blood-thirst as gloated over
the horrors of Dahomey, or has made possible
such butcheries as we have read of in Armenia;
ay, and so we know whence come the possibilities of vice and wickedness in ourselves.

Only, why does it seem " evil "? Why do we
shudder at it, and shrink from it, and feel like
loathing ourselves even for thinking of such
things? Why do not we just live on, in whatever
life seems natural to us? Whence comes this
sense of good, this admiration for the good,
which shames the evil in us, even while it still
is in us? What is it makes us long for something
better, and keep on hoping that some day we may
attain the better? And, when we look out from
ourselves, to what Goodness is to the heart of
mankind, — all the way from the first dim sense
of law and right to the very highest moral heroism and devoted self-sacrifice, — whence comes
all that?

Yes! That is the mystery, the everlasting mystery of the world: how comes Goodness?

There are some thinkers who fancy that, in
some way, it could be and must have been developed out of the struggle for self. I do not

think we are ever really going to trace it that way. We might get a certain prudential, mutual care that way, but not unselfish love. I do not think any philosophizing is ever going to get real love for others out of any combination or manipulation of love for self. A truer thought seems that idea held by some, and notably worked out in Prof. Henry Drummond's " As cent of Man," that, even from the very beginnings of life, we find not only the unmistakeable struggle for self, but also germs of altruism, care for other life, and that out of these have grown the various developments of goodness. That looks more likely. But that does not explain the mystery, only puts it back a little further. Whence come these germs of care for other life, with such potentialities of all unselfish virtue, up to the loftiest goodness? Ah! here is where the mystery tends to higher things, and points man upward to meanings, and a Power at work which means them, which, however it may seem lost in almost endless trains of causation, leads us, at last, not to mere lifeless " energy," but to some beneficent Power which has caused things to be thus, and is ever silently leading them on.

I think there are few things more interesting in the world than to watch the dawning of this mysterious goodness here and there, and to trace its growth to higher and nobler developments. It may be far short of man in its beginnings. How one would like, for instance, in this matter of the law of kindness, to trace the beginning of all kindness and care for the weak and ailing and poor. All through the animal world the social instinct seems to be to destroy the weak or maimed of the herd or the flock, that is the instinct of such social organisation as they have. Yet even then, as an individual feeling, we find the dawnings of sympathy and help; and stories of animals helping each other in some injury or need are among the noblest pages in natural history. I shall never forget what an old friend once told me of how he used to watch two toads in his greenhouse. One of them had had its foot injured, and could barely crawl about; and he said it was such a touching thing to see the other waiting upon it, and helping it so tenderly over the rough rockery, just as a man might help his lame comrade up some mountain path. Now, how did that individual helpfulness for a poor, maimed creature take the further step of using the social organism to keep such weakness alive instead of destroying it? Ah! who can tell? That is part of the mystery of goodness. Probably, by the time that further stage was reached,

Man was well on the way. And every step of man, each moral advance, first in individual feel ing, then in idea and law, and gradually grow- ing into something of accordant action, is touched with the same element of mystery and wonder. Trace up the gradual law of mutual right and justice, from the wild, measureless instinct of revenge, first, to the restraint of equal vengeance, "an eye for an eye," "for a tooth" only "a tooth," then on to compensation for the injury instead of mere retaliating injury, and onward still to the far higher thought of generosity to an enemy. We cannot trace it. Only, here and there, along the line of growth, we see the new thought manifested in some action which at the moment, perhaps, seemed mere folly to those about, but which has lived in human mem- ory ever since. So, for instance, when David had the sleeping King Saul in his power, that half- mad foe, who was hunting him for his life, and his companion, Abishai, would have pinned the king to the ground with one spear-stroke, "Let me smite him," he said, "and I will not need to smite him a second time!" Ah! in that re- fusal to harm him there is the flashing out of a new standard of kindness, even to enemies!

> "So, age by age, since time began,
> We see the steady gain of man."

And each gain, when it first struck upon the heart of those used to lower ways, must have been a mystery, and the whole onward growth a larger, further-reaching mystery, until it came to its crowning height in that strong Son of Man who seemed to his followers so good, so "godly" in a fashion passing the sons of men, that Paul, in his letter, called him the very "mystery of godliness," that had been manifested not in word or law, but in the very flesh of one made like to his brethren, and yet so far above them.

All this comes to us in that deep word, of Paul's awe at what seemed to him Christ's perfect and mysterious goodness. And it seems to me to put the mystery there forever, not in the evil in man and in the world, but in goodness, from its lowest manifestation up to its very highest.

But now, finally, what does all this amount to? Does it make goodness easier, thus to recognise it as the deep, divine mystery of the world?

I do not know that it does, in any single act of life. But I think it does help the good in our nature and the good in the world. It helps us not to be quite so despairing when the evil seems as if it was pervading all and carrying all before it. It helps us to be patient even with evil, to understand that goodness grows slowly in the divine evolution of the world, but that it does grow, always has been growing, and is not going to cease and come to a stand still now.

No: it may not make any visible change when some dire temptation comes upon the heart, or some wild passion rises like a whirlwind within us. It is not any moralising or philosophising that helps us then, but just whatever near motive of love or honor there may be to cling to. But life is not all crises of hot temptation; and meanwhile, in quieter and evener times, it is a help to life's better growth to recognise this deep, mysterious force of good which holds us and will not let us utterly go, and which, the more we think of it, the more we know that it will never let us have peace in any wrong. Yes: the sense of this, the thought of this, is something to help the good in us, to help us in the daily living for life's nobler things; and it is something to help us, even in all our conscious weakness, never to give up the strife or to despair of trying again; to make us sure that God has not forsaken us or given us up, so that we may not give ourselves up. Yes; and, apart from our own personal struggle, it should help us to keep up the struggle in the world for justice and right among nations, and for the uplifting of the fallen and despairing, and for all social well-being. And so the nobler life is kept still strengthening among men, and kindness grows from a personal to a social ideal; and the world keeps moving round a little out of the ancient darkness. It is not yet into any perfect light it comes; but, at least, it comes where we can see dawning the lights of God's higher meanings for man, and so we can keep on watching and waiting and striving and praying, and know that his world is moving and that the Day will come.

THE MYSTERY OF PAIN

IF GOD is good and if he is all powerful, why is it that the world has these dire shapes of pain and sorrow and death among its constant presences? If the Infinite is Love, why is it that no moment of no hour, the centuries through, but bears out into the Infinite some groan or shriek or curse of life writhing in the grasp of some overmastering calamity? Even in the animal world it seems bad enough, and students of nature like Huxley and John Fiske have declared Nature to be full of cruelty and a scene of incessant and universal strife. In human life the agony seems even more acute. Of all the multitudes of the living, not one but has some pang to bear. Some hearts are worn almost to despair by all life's burden and pain. To all, in a few brief years, the sun will darken and the light of life go out, with pangs the sum of which, as one thinks of the myriads of earth's people, is awful to compute. Why is it? If God is good and is all power, why is all this? This is " the mystery of pain."

Do you suppose that I think I can explain it all? No, but I do think that there are some lights upon it here and there which show it as not quite such a hopeless mystery as is often alleged — lights which point towards predominant beneficence as to a mystery not to blind, lifeless forces, but of a slowly working goodness, a mystery not disintegrating things into chaos, but rounding them toward ever higher order; — a mystery therefore, not of atheism and despair, but of faith and hope and quiet immovable trust.

The first light which strikes me on this subject of pain is as to the real proportions of the mystery. We are apt to exaggerate it. We exaggerate it by the very fact of massing it together in our thought, in order to get a completer view of it. But it is not a completer view. That is not how Nature distributes pain. It is really mixed up with a great deal of happiness. Take, for instance, this thought of evolution. I am told of a thousand or a million perishing for one " fittest " to survive. But then, that does not take place all at once, as one dire tragedy of slaughtered. That struggle for existence is simply the name we give to the whole life of animated nature, viewed in the light of its large result of gradual change and progress. Every element of it is going on all the time — in the trees above your head, where the birds seem having a pretty good time upon the whole, and in the grass where the insects live their little life, and in the waters in which the tiny fish are playing in their shoals. Some are dying all the time, and the types are changing as the centuries roll. And yet it does not strike us as such a dreadful spectacle. Have you ever thought how seldom in your country walks, for instance, you see a dead animal, — so seldom that you always stop to look at it. For all those birds of which you see a thousand busy and happy in every mile or two, how often is it that you find one lying dead? The preying of animals — preying on one another — sounds very cruel; but it is very doubtful how much pain there is about it. My friend Crowther Hirst has for some years been making inquiries as to the actual pain felt, even by the most sensitive of animals, man, when he is preyed upon by the greater wild beasts; and the result is a curious consensus of testimony that the shock of a lion's or tiger's onslaught seems to numb the system, almost taking away all pain, even when leaving consciousness. Of course I do not mean that there is no pain in the natural world, but that many things point to its being so spaced out in general happy life as not to be any unbearable mystery. And is it not really a good deal so with the pain of mankind when you look at it in its real perspective in the whole of life? It, too, is mixed up with a good deal of happiness. On the whole, man would rather live than not.

Indeed, pain is so mixed up with enjoyment in its actual happening, that, as a fact, the world at large has never been either crushed or hopelessly perplexed by it. Because, we must remember, it is not we who have first experienced this mystery of pain. From the beginning the very same facts which perplex us have pressed upon the life of man; and yet on the whole mankind have felt that it is not a bad world to live in. Individuals may have been pessimists, but not the human race in its average feeling. Individuals may have welcomed suicide as an escape from so bad a world, but never races. And yet in older times all the elements of pain were larger, stronger, in more awful masses, than they are to-day. We are horrified to hear of some dreadful famine. Why, in the older world there were a dozen famines for every one to-day, and far more terrible. We are shocked by the decimations of some pestilence, against which all precautions or remedies seem powerless. The pestilences of the ancient world were infinitely worse. In the Black Death of the fourteenth century a quarter of the whole population of Europe and Asia died. In England and Italy, half the people perished. There were towns and villages in which hardly a soul survived. In those old centuries the plague came almost every generation. And yet, even with such things to average in, mankind in the mass has never doubted either that life is worth living or that God is good. Take the great world-religions. Even those which have felt the power of evil so immense as to regard it as a rival god have believed in the good God, as the strongest. Zoroastrianism — Parseeism now — is the world's most perfect dualism, with Ormuzd, the good Deity, and Ahriman, the power of evil. But in the lapse of countless eaons it was Ormuzd, the power of light and right, who was to triumph. The mystery of pain was in blacker masses and men could not see even as far into it as we can. And yet what they saw was enough to keep alive an indomitable feeling that the balance of result is to the good.

The second light upon the mystery — not explanation of it (that, as I have said, we must not expect) but a sort of light which shows it not quite so dark — is this; that it is not those who are most in the shadow of pain who most feel it a mystery. You see, when I point to that

great fact which I have been dwelling on, that
the mass of mankind do not feel the world so
hopelessly evil, I am apt to be told, No, perhaps
not, because the pain does not fall upon the
whole of mankind at once, and it is easy for
people to be philosophical about the pain of
others. But do you note that that really is an
admission that, leaving aside the sufferings of
others, the generality of lives have not more
suffering of their own than they can face without
dismay? And there is something still more striking about this, namely that it is not even those
who have most to bear who most feel pain such
an oppressive mystery. This is not a matter of
large general averages, for which statistics can
be referred to; but I think, if you go over in
your mind those who have had the heaviest burdens to bear, the most pain, those upon whom the
mystery of pain has most seemed, to others, to
rest — they have not really been the most op-
pressed by it, their faith in God's goodness most
shaken. As far as my experience goes, it has
been the very opposite. Those difficulties of
faith, arising from there being so much pain in
the world, are almost all difficulties of those who
look at it in theory, not of those who practically
have to bear it. In the course of a pretty long
ministry I have seen many, very many, suffer-

ing ones, but for the most part it has been those
suffering ones who have had the happiest faith. It
has been those who have known most of pain
who have least felt it any oppressive mystery.
Why, how often do you see in some crippled
or sorely tried life, almost a special compensation in the beautiful sweetness of character and
soul! Their friends may feel such pain a " mystery," hardly ever they themselves. Col. Inger-
soll said once that the fact of one martyr was
enough to discredit the idea of a good God.
But, if there were any real force in that difficulty, how curious that the martyrs themselves
have never felt it, for assuredly they have not.
There have been no grander testimonies of tri-
umphant faith in God's goodness than have continually risen from those on whom that mystery
of pain has come in the shape of fierce agonies
of rack or fire. So that practically, this mystery
of pain does not seem to be so hopeless and oppressive as theoretically, one is apt to think it
should be.

But now let us look at it theoretically. Look
at this element of pain as it appears in the whole
make-up of the world. Take Nature for a moment (apart from the idea of God.) Regard
Nature as a mere congeries of forces, or if you
think that science tends toward the idea that all

forces are but variations of the same force, then
regard Nature as the varied manifestation of
one mighty and mysterious energy. We will not
say God, at present, but " energy "; and all that
is, and all the gradual changing and becoming
of things, the outcome of that energy. Well, is
the outcome good? not, is it perceptibly good
in each separate part, — that it is hardly to
be expected we should be able to see — but,
is the general outcome of all these forces
or of this energy good? Is the changing
and becoming of things good? Is the final re-
sultant of all the various intricate working good?
Does the sweep of the whole trend toward good?
Why, who can doubt it? What has the long
past been doing? Think how this globe, to read
its history by the later light of science, has
evolved from the primeval fire-mists into this
wondrous earth, with all the wonder and beauty
of its myriad-fold life! Think of that marvellous ' development ' and all that has come of it,
— for it is all the work of this mighty net-
work of co-operating forces, all, up to man, looking at it, admiring it, investigating it — yes, up
to man, with his sense of goodness and right.
Do not leave out any of the destruction and
death and conflict that there has been. Recognise all the pain that has been involved in this

slow process, which through millions of years
has been bringing all this to pass. But has not
the sweep of the whole been trending unmis-
takeably to good? Is it not a grand order, that
which through whatever clash and conflict there
may have been, has kept all working together in
the subtle endless chain of cause and effect, with
such result as we see in the heavens and the earth
and in the life of man? And then remember
that the pain is simply a part of that order, and
we have got to accept it as it is, this mighty
order with its earthquakes and volcanoes as well
as its roses and its butterflies, with its death ever
changing into life and life ever changing into
death. Shall we say that one part is bad and the
other good? All belong together in the grand order. Shall we complain because the order is often
hard on man? Yet we can see how it is this
very order and the absolute certainty of it, which
has enabled man to take a gradually wiser,
stronger, safer part in the midst of the great
complicated whole. Man might have been a mere
atom in the whole, fitting in like a star or a tree;
but he has a nobler part — a part of growth and
a part of thought — and has had to feel his
way step by step into his part in this intricate
network of substances and forces. And the very
things which have seemed hard upon him have

helped him.   Suffering has been his greatest teacher.   Pain is simply the educating touch of those great forces around him, when he has taken hold of them wrongly, been ignorant of them, or tried to disregard them.   Science has been his settled knowledge of them; and science has only been possible because they are so settled. Once a force known, a law known, known for ever!   And the more man keeps it, the more he finds it beneficent.

Well now change the terms.   Instead of saying Nature or energy, let us say God.   This mysterious something that causes all things to be — from the primeval fire-mist all the way up to man — and all to be bound, and to work, so wondrously together— instead of calling this "Order" or "Tendency" or "lifeless Force" let us think of it as mind and will, working in and through all things.   But is anything altered? Is anything worsened?   Is the great order which we call "Nature" and which we see to be bene ficent if man uses it rightly, — is it less bene ficent if we regard it as the product of an intelligence which meant it?   Surely we shall not regard that as evil in God which we have just been admiring as good in Nature!   And yet that is just what people often do!   It is only a little while ago that I was reading one of these modern diatribes against religion, founded upon this fact of the mystery of pain. The writer spoke of all the pain and misery of the world as so dreadful that, if there were a God who permitted it, he must be a sort of fiend; and then with a final burst of indignation he said, "From such religion I turn away; I turn to Nature and Science" — in the very next paragraph he began extolling the calm, unchangeable order of Nature. But surely there is no real sense in that! It is playing fast and loose with the meaning of facts to denounce them as the will of God and then to praise them as the outcome of Nature. No! This is one of the great gains which have come of Science: it has taught us to feel that man's real hope is in the mighty unchangeable order of the laws that cause the whole, not in some impossible suspension or relaxation of those laws. So all this pain of the world is man's teacher to a better future; and, while thus teaching man, it has not, as I showed at first, ever been practically enough really to discourage or dismay mankind.

You notice that I do not put this use, as man's teacher, as *the* explanation of the mystery of pain; but I think it is a light upon it, making it look not so dark. But there is a greater light still, I think, in seeing how this liability to

danger and pain provides the world with its intensest moral impulses. It is out of dangers and
calamities that the noblest heroism of the world
is born. Accidents, perils, destructions, which at
first almost strike you dumb by the awfulness
of the pain they involve, are constantly found to
arouse a courage, a heroism, which lift them clear
out of the rank of mere physical events and
give them a value to the world's higher life, utterly outweighing all mere bodily suffering. You
know how there is never a railroad accident, a
ship-wreck, a great fire, never any one of those
dire catastrophes in which the mystery of pain
seems to come to its very climax, but out of the
dark mystery gleams some light of beautiful he-
roic unselfishness. Take an illustration. I recall
the most awful colliery explosion that ever took
place in England, that at the " Oaks " Colliery
in 1866, in which above three hundred men and
boys perished. But that was not all. While it
was still doubtful if some might not be saved,
there was a call for volunteers to go down; and
without a moment's hesitation thirty-three men in
all went down, and at their head the gallant
young engineer, Parkin Jeffcock. And then a
little while of waiting, and suddenly another explosion, the very gearing of the pit blown into
shapeless ruins; and not only was all hope for

the main body of miners at an end, but every one of those explorers had perished too.

I knew that part of the country in those days, and I remember as if it were but yesterday how the horror of all that thrilled through the country; and one of the very thoughts it set many thinking was just this; How could such a thing happen, if there be a good God? And yet, how not? That first calamity was simply the penalty of some careless handling of the mighty forces concerned. I believe it came out afterwards that the men had made one long blast to serve instead of two shorter ones, and that, in a coal-seam in which a liberal keeping of nature's requirement would have excluded all blasting. I see no " mystery " there, simply the lesson on a terribly large scale to keep more loyally the law of those things which are so freely given to man to use. But the loss of those brave explorers? And yet, in reality, is not that the noblest element in the whole story? Yes, that they should offer themselves, that they should face the risk for their fellows. But then, would not a good God have taken care of them and kept them harmless? Where would be the heroism if some divine protection were in the habit of holding such " forlorn hopes " unscathed?

Let us have more trust — the very kind of

trust these men had. For what was their trust?
That the fire and poisonous gas and caving rock
could not hurt them or kill them when on such
an errand? No; but that, if they were on such
an errand, death itself was not a thing to fear
or shun or trouble about. And so it is. I can
feel pity for those three hundred men blown to
death while at their ordinary work, because it
seems such a needless, pitiful waste of life that
had no business ever to have happened. But,
for those thirty-three who were there upon that
noble, unselfish errand, I feel pity to be utterly
out of place. No, for this is not a play world
in which the sternest dangers are make-believes,
and a good natured God waits round to keep his
best children, at least, from getting hurt or killed.
It is a world of hard realities, and awful, unswerving forces; and the goodness of that mighty
Life that works through it is seen, not in some
occasional kind checking of those forces, but in
this — that, awful and unswerving as they are,
they work for good, in nature toward beauty and
use, in man toward fuller knowledge and wiser
working; and even at the awfullest, to the loftiest
intensity of human character.

And yet one thing more, to end with. If you
wish for the very happiest and clearest light
upon that mystery of pain you will find

it, not even by any way of bearing it or
looking at it, but by going right into it and
trying to make it a little less. The problem that
seems to defy your logic becomes, I do not say
transparent, but at least full of light to loving
helpfulness. I hardly know how it should be so;
but, certainly I have never known anyone who
has taken firm hold of this problem of pain and
who is spending any part of his or her days in
really grappling with it and trying here and
there to lessen it and heal it — I have never
known such an one to feel any oppressive difficulty about it. It is those who look on it
from the outside, it is those who muse over it
in their studies, to whom pain seems to lie upon
the world like a black impenetrable cloud. Go
into that cloud and you find that in and out of it
come a thousand glints of light and use and
beautiful, hopeful meaning. There, not in the
totality of pain as you observe it, but in its in-
dividuality as you try to help or heal it, you
begin to understand its wise beneficent part in
the slow, onward development of man. There,
trying to help or heal, it comes to you how your
loving desire is but a tiny impulse of the great
meaning of the whole — that whole which works
not only through dead forces, but through living
hearts, and means not the forces only, which

often we cannot understand, but the hearts and the hearts' love which we can understand. And so, as you go patiently on, doing your little part in the helping and the healing, there comes a sense of how the threads, both of our working and our thinking, lose themselves in the vast weavings of eternal things. And here we are only among beginnings, but beginnings that keep moving on; and so the mysteries and fears and tremblings of earth and man lose themselves, not in chaos and darkness, but in that infinite meaning and infinite beneficence which our hearts adore as " God."

LIFE ON THE LINE OF LEAST RESISTANCE

IT IS one of the great laws of the material world that all movement must take place along the line of least resistance. Some of the thinkers of our day maintain that this is equally true of our human living, and that it is right for it to be so. It does not seem exactly the Master's Counsel, indeed; "Go in at the narrow gate," he puts it, "not at the wide one;" that is — "Take the hard way, not the easy one."

Which is right? It is worth a little looking into. You know in the present time there is a great liking for large generalizations, which may include nature and man in one category and one law. This is just one of those generalizations — and it is worth looking into to see whether it is true — or whether there is some higher element in man that will not arrange itself with these material forces, but requires some higher explanation and seems to depend on some higher law.

First of all let us get a clear idea of what

237

this law is, of all movement having to be on the line of least resistance. Watch it in its very simplest illustrations. Pour a little water on the ground and notice what becomes of it. Its little streams move slowly in this or that direction as if feeling about. What are they feeling for? Simply for the lines of least resistance — the direction in which there is least to obstruct its flow. But it is not only in such a slow movement as that of water that we can trace this law. When a gun is fired, the force of the explosion is really equal all round, but it is obliged to find its outlet by the barrel because that is the line along which there is least resistance. So when a steam boiler bursts, the direction of the explosion is settled by the same law. It seems a simple matter these little trickles of water feeling for a slight descent, or this expansive force breaking out at the weakest point. But as you watch these things you see in operation, one of the mighty laws which have helped to mould and to develop the universe. These planets find their circling orbit through the vast world-spaces, not in a perfect circle, but just where the balancing and counteracting attractions of sun and stars leave the least resistance to that unknown force which impels them on. The great air-currents by which the signal service watchers fore-

cast a storm or the rise or fall of temperature, il-
lustrate the same law. Nor is this only the
principle of movement for dead matter. Examine the winding twisting fibres at the root of
a tree. Those tiny cells that keep being added
at the extremity insinuate themselves through
the interstices of the soil, or the crannies of the
rock in search of moisture just where at each
point there is the least resistance. In reality, it
is probable that this principle is operating in
every movement of animated nature, from the
swerving aside of a runaway horse if you try to
stop it, to the slow, gradual changes of place,
food and habit, which, through the long cycles
of human time, have regulated the course of development and the survival of the fittest. Herbert Spencer, from whom some of these illustrations are borrowed, traces this principle right
onward into human action, too, and believes that
it both explains man's past and conditions his
future. There, however, the questioning comes
in.

Let it be frankly admitted that the law of
" Life on the line of least resistance " does interpret a good deal of human action — It is very
interesting to trace it. It interprets all that part
of life in which man is still simply one of the
animals. The struggle to supply the animal

wants, the first groupings of society, the large, hardly conscious movements of peoples — all follow this law. Man stands in the midst of the vast nature, needing to live and having to put forth his powers in order to obtain food, clothing, warmth, safety. Nature more or less resists his efforts. A sort of antagonistic pressure surrounds him. Man's life tends to those ways, to those places, where this pressure is least. Thus the sheltered valleys are peopled before the bleak hills or plains. Thus population spreads along sea shore, where there is always food for the catching. Thus migration takes place from countries where life is difficult to those where it is easy. Human industry flows to those occupations in which, as we say there is most room and in which, consequently, life's wants are supplied with least difficulty. So with the lines of human communication. The primitive roads over moor and fell and the carefully planned railroad across a country, are alike directed by the line of least resistance.

So far then we trace the law, through inanimate matter and through animated Nature up to man; and even in man's doings where those doings are impersonal, in large sweepings of tendency or movement which are independent of individual will; in fact we trace this law till we come to doings which depend on individual will and personal character. But there we have to pause. When we come to man's free, individual life, the law no longer holds, at least not in the same way. It no longer holds as a self-acting, automatic law, dominating man without any consciousness on his part. The fact that man's life is conscious introduces quite a new factor. The question arises: is this law of motion along the line of least resistance a law which man ought to set before himself? and I cannot look out on man's common life without feeling that it is not. It may seem curious that as soon as man comes to his own voluntary life, he should have to break away from the law which has brought him so far, but so it is. From the moment man becomes a self-conscious being, thinking of his own actions and of the right and wrong of them — from that moment, no more life merely on the line of least resistance. From that moment all the further progress of life and all the dignity and moral worth of life may be said to depend on his living, not on the line of least resistance but almost the contrary. Of course it is not so absolutely. The moral value of an action can be no more decided absolutely by its being hard than by its being easy; but certainly the idea of the true thing being to look out for the easy way is scattered to the winds. And mark, this is not because the terms no longer apply. The terms do apply, they fit with a curious aptitude. That idea of acting on the line of least resistance is very easy to translate into life, but it gives the wrong sort of life. You can see plenty of applications of it, parallels for almost every illustration I have given from Nature. Take that of water on the ground, feeling about for its line of least resistance. Have you never seen that in life? People whose whole course is just that limp feeling about for the easiest way; who are always trying to get along with the minimum of effort and trouble, who endeavour to dodge round every difficulty and obstacle? There is your "life on the line of least resistance," only it is the wrong kind of life. When a man gets into a passion and instead of venting it on some equal, who would talk back, vents it on his errand-boy or his dog — that is passion on the line of least resistance — but it certainly does not make the passion better. Yes, it is very easy to understand, and dreadfully easy to carry out, this physical law, but it is pretty poor to set up as a law of life, for it gives the wrong kind of life every time. No lack of opportunity for seeing how it works, for a great deal of the life of the world is lived exactly on this principle. Every man who puts off till to-morrow what he ought to do to-day; every man who sits at home with his slippers on when he ought to go to a committee or a meeting; every business man who shirks balancing his books because of what he is afraid to find confronting him there; every politician who trims his principles to stave off awkward opposition — all these are exact illustrations of acting on the line of least resistance. And this is not the poorest kind of the life it leads to. The confirmed idler who does not do what he ought either to-day or to-morrow; the tramp who slips into mendicancy because begging is easier than working; the criminal who slips into thieving because thieving is easier than either working or begging — all these are fair actual illustrations, of trying to continue into the free life of man, the principle of movement on the line of least resistance.

On the other hand, all that is great, all that is noble, all that is progressive in man's life, has been attained not along that line, but quite independent of it; often along the exactly opposite line. The story of all great achievements, of all lives steadfastly pursuing noble ends, of all reforms wrought through tribulation and disappointment to final victory, has ever been the story of men choosing not the easier way, but the harder, and finding it, mostly, even harder than they dreamed, and still holding right on. When Huss and Wycliffe began the movements which, a century or more later, were to become the Reformation — well, Reformation, even in Luther's time, with all the increased prepared- ness of the world was hardly a movement on the line of least resistance — (it would have been easier to have let it alone, even then) but what was it in its beginnings, when the resistance was so fierce that it brought Huss to the stake and scattered Wycliffe's desecrated ashes to the winds? And you see the same thing when you look at life now, in any of its stronger, nobler, aspects. It is not along the line of least re- sistance that poor lads have forced their way to fortune, and dwellers in humble garrets strug- gled into fame; or that the patient workers of Science have groped and dug their way into the deep and secret lore of Nature. No! Even the busy mother, who is beset by a hundred cares to keep the home things sweet and comely, and sometimes feels as if it would be such a relief to give it all up and let everything go, but never does, — that is not life along the line of least resistance.

And see! All this is not affected by the fact that there are other resistances besides those

which people see at the moment, and which often
make what seems to begin with, the easiest way,
eventually the hardest. I know it. " The way
of transgressors is hard " — at least, it is going
to be. And the way of the righteous is going
to be easier by and bye, though it would be difficult to make out that it is, ever, the easiest. But
this does not touch the question. If you want
to know whether this natural law in the lower
level of things is also to be the law man should
hold up before himself, watch the law as it is.
These further resistances and readjustments are
precisely what the natural law takes no account
of. Does the water, when it comes to the edge
of a slight depression, abstain from going down
because a little way on the ground rises again
so that there is no real outlet that way? No.
And so your easy going procrastinator who
shirks his work to-day, even though he knows
perfectly well it will be harder to-morrow, is a
true parallel, not a sham one. Only, that which
is right and good for the water is wrong and
bad for the man. Even in those human en-
terprises in which the line of least resistance is
the actual desideratum, man's agency at once
introduces a new and higher element. The en-
gineers, cutting a line of railway have to seek
the line of least resistance; but they have to do so

on the survey of the whole country and often must choose the more difficult way to begin with, in order to avoid some worse obstacle further on. The fact is, the moment you touch man's life, a whole set of higher principles comes in; and what we need to do is to keep those higher principles foremost in our thought; and to try to explain them in the terms of something quite lower is not to help us but to confuse us. Not what is the line of least resistance, but what is the line of right, is the thought really to guide us. Even if it could be shown that in some final working out of things, the line of right will turn out also to be that of least resistance, that does not help, because that line will still only be found by looking out for the right. But it cannot be shewn; and every thought of it only distracts and weakens our hold upon the simple consideration of right. There is a poor fellow, for instance, in some sore temptation. He is hesitating on the threshold of some sin, and the way is dreadfully open, and every fibre of his senses is enticing him in. Yet he is trying to rally his soul to the right. Go to him and tell him that the law of the Universe is, to choose the line of least resistance. Can you undo the demoralising effect of such a word by any argument to shew that what you mean is, that the path of eventually least resistance is away from that temptation? Or go to some struggling reformer, whose life year after year has been one long battling against the stream — and try your philosophy on him. "My friend, the real law of life is to choose the line of least resistance." Why, if he believes you, he will be halfway down stream, drifting with the current and finding it so easy — before you can reach him with even the first word of your explanation that he should still go struggling on, up-stream, because *there* he would eventually find that "least resistance." Do you not see? You fancy you have got a great beautiful generalisation which proclaims itself a sort of universal law, and lo! the moment you try to apply it practically, it leads you to weakness and confusion, and so far as you think of it at all, it is a principle rather to avoid than to follow.

It all comes simply to this: that all these attempts to make the higher life of man clearer by referring back to mere material things, as if they were a little more reliable, are vain; and so we are thrown back upon the higher life itself, and its own consciousness, and the great expressions of it in these grand old-world teachings of simple right; and all these come back with a new emphasis and power. This moral consciousness of mankind, which has kept growing with man's growth, developing as part of his development, is just as certain as his physical science. The higher things may not be as exactly definable, as the lower; but they are quite as real and in the main lines of them just as clear.

Every now and then along the ages there comes a sort of chill over the ancient trust and faith of man, in all that higher life. It has been so to some extent, in this past generation. The sharp clear light of science has flamed up, and the old moral and religious lights of the world have seemed a little dim and uncertain in the new electric glare. Science has become so wonderful and withal has revealed its truths in such sharp clear outline, and such hard palpable reality, that it has seemed sometimes as if its truths and laws must be about to take the place of those vague old-fashioned laws of the moral life and of the vague undefined sentiments of religion.

But no. The further we go on, the further science itself goes on, the more we find that there is something in the life of man different from anything and everything else. Try how you will to generalise man's life into line with mere material nature, you cannot do it. You can generalise a part of man on the material line, and that so thoroughly that you are tempted to think the whole of him might be treated so — but simply, when you have done all you can, whole realms of man's being remain out of line. Before the struggle with temptation, before the grief of Penitence, before the self-sacrifice of Love, the laws of matter which we try to fit to everything, fall, helpless and meaningless.

And so in these greater things of life, we have to go back to the old light and the old helpers. Here, in the old ways and the old words, in which our fathers and long centuries of struggling men strengthened their hearts to bear their burdens and to do their duty — here is the light to guide us still, and most of all it is in Him, above all others, who has been the very Light of the World. From all that thought which would try to find some all embracing law of life in the physical law of movement on the line of least resistance, I turn back again to the old counsel of the Master to seek rather the harder way and to distrust that line of least resistance, the "broad and pleasant way," as a way that "leadeth to destruction."

Yes; "enter ye in at the strait gate," the "hard and narrow way," It is not the line of "least resistance," and no logic of generalisation can make it that for any practical guidance; but it is the line of right; it is the line of real on-

ward life; it is the line of a peaceful conscience
and a quiet heart; and as you go on in it, its
hardness shall grow less, its grade less steep, and
if you will go on in it, and keep on patiently,
you shall find the truth of that other grand word,
that "the pathway of the just is as the shining light, that shineth more and more unto the
perfect day."

ONE OF THE MEANINGS OF GREAT CATASTROPHES

WHAT about that terrible famine in India, what about the Java eruption? How do these great calamities which come simply from the operation of the mighty laws and forces of Na ture, mostly apart from any responsibilty of man — how do these fit in with the idea of the eternal goodness? Most of what men call accidents — fires, shipwrecks, and so forth — we can in a sense understand. They are mostly the penalty of broken law, of some carelessness in the handling of those mighty edge-tools, the forces of Nature. They are educators, stern but beneficent, — beneficent by their very inexorableness. If we are to use steam or electricity, it is best that the power of them should be absolute — so we know what we are doing. But the great natural catastrophes and destructions are different. When some twenty years ago that awful tide-wave swept the coast of India for hundreds of miles, destroying some quarter of a million lives —

no human foresight could have done much to lessen the horror. And now in this terrible famine — over extents of country about equal to the whole of France — Why, foresight might perhaps have made more provision of water or food than it has done — though I believe the irrigation of India is better on the whole than ever before, but still in the large sweep of it, it was quite beyond human forecast or prevention. And what is the meaning of it all? How it all comes right in face of our worship of an Infinite goodness; our words about God's faithful providence, all the old words, that men have been saying or singing since the Psalmist's time, of trust in God's tender care! It forces back upon us the question whether we use words that have no real meaning? Is that old thought of a gracious providence, all a mistake? Is this world really in the hold of some blind force or forces, to which our safety and happiness, our cries and tears, are all alike indifferent? No! I do not think we feel so. "Though he slay me, yet will I trust in Him." Our faith in God is not of yesterday. Our sense of the general beneficence of things, of the trend of good in the vast order which has evolved and is always evolving the world, is too strongly based to be really or permanently endangered by any bewilderment at parts of the great process which we cannot understand. But even though people may reassure their souls, that it must surely be right and good on the whole, they still cannot help feeling the bewilderment. They crave for some light, some meaning in such a calamity.

If it does not mean passionless indifference, what does it mean?

I am no prophet, to interpret to you such things as this, and to say why the Almighty power and wisdom suffers such irregularities to come even in the working out of his most trusted seasons. I cannot stand here and say: This or this is the meaning of the Infinite Life, in such things. No. And yet as I think it all over, and over again—there is one little side-light of meaning which does seem to appear — not any explanation of such calamities, not why they are; no, — but one meaning which they seem to flash out upon us as they go along.

I can put the whole thing in a single sentence. I said just now, that such a shock of widespread failure or destruction makes us ask — does it mean that the Great Father-life of the universe does not care for us? No, it does not mean that — but it does seem to mean that He does not care much for our bodies! It does seem to mean that in is great world-plan the body — that, remember, which man is always concerning himself most about, is in God's sight comparatively nothing, hardly worth taking into account, not worth stepping aside for. It is the higher life in it, what we call the soul, God seems to care for. The body has just to take its chance (so to speak) among the other things of earth.

Now, this is something worth looking into. Take, first, man's thought, the relative value man is apt to set on his body and on his soul, and then we begin to see the significance of the very different proportion in which the divine world-plan seems to hold them.

One cannot look out into the world, without seeing that what man feels most of in himself, believes in most, cares infinitely the most for is — the body. Men generally, believe that they have souls, but the body is what they really seem to live for. I am not speaking of bad men; but of how average human life lives this way. The whole arrangements of ordinary life are those of beings who feel that the real substantial thing, is, to enjoy this present life, to get together all that is possible of its good each year. It is by success or failure in this that men take their rank in earthly society. Indeed, by " success " or "failure " men almost always mean success or failure in bodily earthly things.

" What is a man worth "?   Means — how much
material treasure?   Even the very charities
and kindnesses of the world, evince the same
thing.   They look to the bodily life more than
to anything else.   Men do not like to see their
fellows suffering cold or hunger, living amid
unwholesomeness and dirt, or in sickness or disease.   Those are the " problems " which weigh
upon " society."   Yet all the time, there are
infinitely sadder things — and that, among people who are neither starving, nor ragged, nor
dirty — who in every bodily respect are as well
off as need be — but whose real being, in the
innermost fact of it, is starved, and ragged, and
steeped in uncleanness worse than any outward
dirt.   And as you see this in men's ways of using life, so you see it in their way of looking
at sickness and death.   To most people, sickness seems so much taken off from their available life, — and when death, as we call it, comes,
that seems like the end of anything worth really
reckoning as life.   People may talk about the
joys of immortality, but what the most really
want, is, to keep hold, to the uttermost moment
possible, of the body's life, here among the
things of earth.   Anything, even for a few days
more of it, — or even a few hours   That is
why men feel these catastrophes and destructions

of the bodily life so great a trial to their trust in God. Men do not distrust God because they see men sinning. A whole city full of souls, may be, as to many of them, in a state sadder than death, and the religious life goes on with its prayer and uplook as usual. But let a hundred or two bodies be suddenly maimed or destroyed, and straightway there is a widespread shuddering at the horror of it, and men begin crying out — how can a good God let such things be? Yes; there it is; it is life in its bodily, earthly frame and use, that people think of first and last. It is this they see, and care for in themselves, this to which they most minister in others; it is for getting more out of this they spend their strength; it is for the general happiness of this that they extol God's goodness; it is the calamities of this which most trouble their faith, it is for the sparing of this a little longer that they lift up the most agonized prayers.

There it is that there comes in this lesson which — I do not say is what God means to teach, but which certainly does appear out of these great calamities. It seems as if they put it to us, sometimes with startling, and almost cruel plainness, that our estimate of the body and the bodily life, is all wrong, at any rate that

it is not the estimate that Nature, and the Lord
of Nature, put upon it. Why, we might learn
this, from the very place our bodies hold in the
universe. They just have to stand or fall, with
the common run of earthly things. They are
of the earth, earthy. Nay, if they were man's
all, the case is even worse. Man has hardships
and difficulties of which the brutes know
nothing. All things point to bodily happiness as what the brutes are created for, but
they do not point so in man's case. They
have their wants supplied with less labour,
more as a part of the natural working of things,
than man has. What a different spectacle — the
birds going forth in the morning to get their
daily bread, and men and women going forth to
get theirs. What do birds know of the strain
of care? The ordering of nature in the matter
of wholeness and health tells the same story,
— seems to show that with other creatures, the
body is the dominant consideration; that, with
man, it is a secondary consideration, subordinate
to, leading up to something else. And this is
what has to be constantly kept in mind. For
the lesson that we learn as catastrophes pass by,
of the comparative unimportance of the body, of
how comparatively little God cares for it, does
not stand alone as a mere negative lesson — No,

it keeps carrying with it the positive lesson, — of the worth and glory of the higher element in man. For see; that providence which seems so curiously indifferent to our bodies, lavishes its finest and most wondrous influences upon the soul. All the divinest power of His Working seems to concentrate itself upon the soul. So, things that with the beasts have only a material, bodily significance, with man have a moral and spiritual use. Labour, and the strain of care — all that side of life which goes to supplying the means of living — are with man (quite above what they are to the beasts) the means of strengthening and developing that higher element of mind, and soul-life. Pain and sickness are almost unknown among animals. If they are crippled or diseased, and when their powers are failing — Nature makes an end of them. But sickness, pain, and the weakening powers of old age are a part of the essential lot of man. God causes human beings to be kept living on for years, in bodily life so weak or painful that animals would not be kept in it for as many days. Why? Because what God is caring for and working for is, the soul. Man's body is his for the sake of the soul; and long after it has become a poor, pleasureless thing considered as a body, it still may do for the soul to live and grow in, and in-

deed its very pain and helpfulness may be helpful discipline for the soul.   So nature — through
human instinct and feeling, if you will — lets
man live on, even provides for his being helped
to live on, long after the animal would have been
mercifully put out of its misery.

It is simply the same fact — a sort of divine
indifference to the body part of man, which
comes out in these destructions.   Here are we —
thinking so much of our bodies, toiling for them,
studying how to pamper them, guarding them
so carefully from every wound or pain, — and
meanwhile God's working in the earth sweeps on,
and takes no more notice of our bodies than
of so many flies.   Sometimes it is one that per-
ishes in some sweep of force, sometimes a dozen
at once — now and then hundreds; — once in
years comes some giant catastrophe that destroys
half a people and sends a shudder through the
whole race.   " Can God be good? " men cry
— but all goes impassively on.   His mighty
forces turn neither to the right hand nor the
left.   Again, it is not that He does not care
for us, no, but apparently that He does not
care much for our bodies.   But here is the unit-
ing truth: it seems as if He does not count these
bodies to be *us:* only the temporary clothing of
us.

Long ago when I was living among the great cotton factories there was a great sensation among the workpeople, for an accident that had happened. A man had been cleaning some machinery while it was going, and the great revolving strap had caught his shirt sleeve, and — no! it had not drawn him in; his clothing was old and worn, and simply it had dragged it in, and stripped every rag of it off him, and left him standing there as naked as he was born!

Was he sorry that his clothes were poor and worn? Nay, rather thankful, that it was they that went and not he. And so it may be that God does not count these bodies to be us; it is not these bodies that He is Father to, and loves, and cares for. Even the body, indeed, is a wonderful thing; and yet what a mere rough affair it is, compared to that wonderful life that dwells in it, and uses it, and is its motive power. And as he has made this soul-life the most wonderful, so He deals the most wonderfully with it. All that tenderness of individual care which we are often disappointed that He does not have for our bodies, He does have for our souls. There, He meets with us spirit to spirit. There it is that we come into our true relation to Him, are conscious of Kinship to Him. And here it is that we find the most subtle, wonderful working of His creating and evolving power. What is the evolution of man's outward body, compared with the evolution of that inward being, of intellect, conscience, affection? These are the greatest things. These are the things that dominate the world. They make up the sphere in which the Infinite spirit touches our souls, responsive to our seeking, with guidance, comfort, strength. The Development is ever upward, and in that development catastrophes are part of the teaching power. When man has yet hardly risen above the beasts, famine is already one of his great teachers, sending him to the river borders, teaching him prudence, foresight, lifting him from the wild comrade-ship of the desert, to the ordered civilisation of the Nile. As he grows still upwards, and learns to ward off much of the original calamity and destruction, what yet remains of it, forms the occasion and the incentive to the very noblest developments of character.

This, then, I might almost put as one of the higher meanings of great catastrophes, — not merely the negative meaning of how the great Power that causes us to be does not seem to care much for our bodies — yet far more is the lesson of the exceeding preciousness of the higher life, our life as souls, and the way these things draw life into closer brotherhood and lift it to its intensest power and grandest height, and help to nurture the finest nobleness of the world.

IMMORTALITY, WHETHER WE WISH
FOR IT OR NOT

ALWAYS as I read how as Jesus was in the way "there came one running, and kneeled to him and asked him — 'Good Master, what shall I do that I may inherit eternal life.'" It is not so much the question, as the wish which evidently prompted the question, that strikes me   This man evidently wished for eternal life, or he would not have asked Christ so eagerly how to attain it.   He "came running" and Kneeled down" to him — those staid, solemn Jews did not run unless they were in dead earnest!   So that it is a good illustration of the wish for immortality. And I want to consider how far that wish is general, and of how far it has to do with man's belief that immortality is to be.   The subject came to me the other day, as I read in a popular periodical this statement that "men have ceased to wish for immortality."   This was put broadly and confidently, as if there could not be any doubt about it.   " Men have ceased to wish for immortality " — and it was put so, evidently with the idea that that practically settled the matter; that, if men are really ceasing even to wish for it, there is really no ground for believing it.

Now I have thought over this a good deal, and the more I have thought the more I have been impressed with these two things.

1st, that it is a mistake to think that people do not wish to live again — I believe that there is just about as much wish that way, as ever there was; — but that, 2nd, man's wishing or not wishing, has nothing to do with the matter — that immortality is one of those great solemn facts of being which has to be faced, which is going to be, whether we wish for it or not. Let us look, for a moment at these two points. — 1st as to how *it* really *is* about men wishing to live again, or, rather, for that is the deeper truth, to go on living. I imagine that in this matter, mankind are about where they always have been; that the wish never was at all universal, but certainly is not really growing less. Yet I can understand how some people should think it is lessening. Because there is a marked change in the way the whole subject is spoken of. I should be inclined to put it *this* way; that those who do not wish for immortality are a great

deal more free in saying so than they used to be
and that those who still do wish for it, are not
anxious about it, do not profess to be so sure,
are more content to leave the whole subject to
the quiet unfolding of whatever God's will for
us may be. This latter change of feeling is very
marked in our time. Men are less inclined to
dogmatize about what is to be. Formerly, you
know, all was laid down very certainly; to admit a doubt about immortality was shocking;
I can remember the time when a man who should
say — he hoped for immortality but could not
feel sure of it, would have been regarded as almost an infidel. Well, it is not so now. People
have come to see that there can be no absolute,
black and white proof, of any of these deep
spiritual realities — and they are more content
to leave it so. Thus you find many, even deeply
religious people, saying frankly that they are content without proof, content to leave it with God
— simply sure that it will be all right. Often
such people speak of immortality as a hope,
rather than as an accepted, or settled belief.
Well, that is a reverent spirit — and hope is
certainly a wish, even if it is not so eager in its
wishing, as the older way of speaking seemed
to be.

And then while those who do hope for immortality are thus a little less confident in affirming it, those who do not hope or wish for it are much more open and confident in their scepticism than they used to be. *All* doubt and disbelief express themselves to-day with a freedom which is a comparatively new thing. There is more talking, and writing and printing, altogether than there used to be, and specially all this is increased at the smaller end. The great thinkers do not talk or write more than they did 500 years ago, but the small thinkers talk and write a vast deal more And so all the scepticism of our time, all the doubt, all the flippant indifference comes right out. I am not saying it should not do. Perhaps it is better *out* than *in* — but it does come out; and so the casual observer is apt to feel, as if that side of thought had immensely increased; and people like the writer I quoted at first, say confidently, that " Men are ceasing to wish for immortality," when really it is simply that those who do not wish for it are more open and confident in saying so.

The larger point is, however, that too much has always been made of this supposed general wish. It has been constantly treated in arguments on the subject, as if of course every one longs to live again. Now I do not think that this has ever been true. There have always been people to whom it would have been a relief not to have to live again. I believe this about others because I have often felt it so myself. I think there come times in every one's experience — times of depression, times of perplexity, times when life has got into some great moral tangle when it would seem the happiest thing, simply to lie down and have done with it all.

No; I am inclined to believe that in the matter of *wishing* for immortality, mankind are about where they have always been; and that any apparent lessening or weakening of that wish arises partly from men having learned more trust, frankly leaving the whole matter to develope itself as God may will; and, partly, from any doubt or wish not to live again, uttering itself much more freely and openly than of old.

But what comes upon me with most force is, that man's belief in immortality did not spring from any wish for it, has never depended upon men's wishing for it, does not depend upon it now. I do not suppose we can really trace the beginning of this belief among mankind. But when our scientific investigators search back as far as they can, it is not to a wish for another life but rather to a dread of it, that they seem to come. Herbert Spencer thinks that the idea of immortality originated among prehistoric men in the fear that great savage chiefs might not be finally dead after all — might still come back to punish their enemies and to plague the living. They did not want them to live again — they tried to keep them dead and still — but they were afraid they could not. No wish for it — but a feeling —first about their chiefs, and finally spreading to common men — that it had to be! And so, again, there have been times — yes, many times — in the history of religions, when the belief in immortality has been so twisted and distorted, as to become not a joy, but a terror — times when it has hung over men like a cloud — times when they not only did not wish for it but would have been thankful to believe it was all a dream — but, in reality the wishing or not wishing had nothing to do with it — they had to believe it, could not get away from it! Look at India. In that hot, oppressive climate — *life* is about as much as men can bear — the ideal of happy life is, to sit simply doing nothing. And there, in India, had grown up through measureless ages the belief in the transmigration of souls — that the soul would keep on passing endlessly from one form of being to another — no stopping — new life, new work, new weariness for ever. Talk of that having grown out of man's *wish* — why it was the very opposite of man's wish, it was a horror! And so when at last a great prophet rose up among them — Buddha — the essence of his wisdom was that he believed he had found out the way of escape from this endless chain of being! The way of escape from Life — *that* was the Gospel of Buddha! And men eagerly embraced it. Whole nations embraced it. That was their wish — not being, but absence of being. Nobody is quite sure what "Nirvana" exactly means, but if it does not mean actual nothingness, it means something as near to it as possible. But here is the striking thing: men could not get away from their belief in immortality — not even through Buddha! It seemed as if they had escaped from it, but they had not, gradually the belief returned in all its force, and if you look into the Buddhist scriptures and pictures, along the subsequent centuries — they are full of representations of life to come — pictures of Heavens and Hells just as graphic and lurid as anything that you can find in Catholicism. No! they did not wish for Immortality, they wanted to get away from it, but they could not.

And it has been a good deal the same in some forms of Christianity. Christianity, when it has got perverted, has sometimes made the thought of Immortality not a joy, but a terror; not something to be wished for, but something to be dreaded. Why, only think what Calvinism became! — Remember how the old Calvinist divines — two hundred and fifty years ago — used to reason it out that not one soul in five hundred thousand could be saved — the rest, all damned — and they believed it, too. Why, it would have been a mercy to regard the whole thing as ended at death. But no! There must have been very little wishing for it, then — but they felt it was to be, whether they wished for it or not.

And that is the great lesson for ever. Whether we *think,* or whether we *live,* so as to make the thought of living on in another world a joy, or something to dread and shrink from, there it is — just as certain as *to-morrow.* There it is, I say. Apart from all questions as to how it came to be, or whether men desire it or not — here is this sense in man, always growing up in his very nature, and when temporarily swept away, still growing up again — one of those great facts of man's being which are their own sufficient evidence. One or another may not feel it; one or another may doubt it or disbelieve it. You may not be able to establish the sense of it in the individual, but in the large view

— of the race — it is unmistakable. That is where the real argument from the general thought and feeling of man comes in. Not from some general wish for it, but from the practically universal sense of it. That is really what establishes all the great thoughts and convictions of the world! Take that great sense of the difference between right and wrong. That does not rest upon your sense or mine. You or I may sometimes wish that wrong was not wrong; we would like to be free to do it — but that great sense of right and wrong grows up in the very life of the race, and the individual is carried on, in the race. Where the value of the individual thought comes in, is, in this: that, in the individual life which is wholesome, and doing its part well, the great thought comes out clearly; the more a man obeys conscience, the more he finds the sacredness and imperativeness of conscience. — And so it is with regard to immortality. Grant that many do not wish for it, and do not mind saying so. Grant that many more, are less anxious about it, feel difficulties and doubts about it, and are willing to leave it to whatever may prove to be the divine will — all this does not touch the great fact, that as the world's life keeps growing up, it still grows up into this faith; and that as life grows nobler and higher and fuller, it feels, not less but more, that it is only at the beginning of things, and only at the beginning of itself. Said Whittier to a friend: "I cannot feel that there is any end to me." That is the natural feeling in all life that has grown and lived sweetly and naturally on, and come to the world's best. No! it is the poor unearnest, selfish life that does not care whether it lives again; it is the vapid, frivolous life that hardly cares whether it lives, and asks "whether life is worth living." Live the nobler life, live for others, live for truth, live for good, and you will never have any doubt that this life is worth living and not much doubt about living on. In a word, live the immortal life, live now as an immortal being, and you will know the truth of immortality. No! It is only the poorer kind of life that has no wish or care to live again. It grows tired even of this life. Of that kind of life it may seem true that it *is* ceasing to wish for it, only it never did wish for it. But the deeper and better life of the world moves steadily on, as ever, towards more and fuller being, towards further-reaching ends, and principles that want much more than *this* life to come to anything; and as this sense of more and fuller being grows, it widens out into powers and possibilities quite beyond the limits of the earthly life. Yes, apart from any question of wishing, man feels it must be so;

> " Thou wilt not leave us in the dust:
> Thou madest man,—he knows not why,
> He thinks he was not made to die
> And thou hast made him: Thou art just."

— Ah yes, Lord, thou art just! Thou wilt not mock this reaching on towards ever higher things, which Thou hast planted in the very nature of thy children!

That is the element of truth in that old idea of some universal wish for immortality. There never was any such universal wish; the wish for *life to be,* depends partly on what life *is,* or at least is striving to be and often a mean poor life finds even this earthly span too long, and would be glad to be sure there is no more to come. But use the present life for the best that is in it; yes, let there be any element even of striving for the best notwithstanding its failures and its poor low living, and even that very element of wishing for something better will develope that deep underlying sense of this life being a mere beginning, a fragment with something more to come! Yes, even the merest fragmentary striving for the best, does so much; but let that striving be the steady purpose of the life, and at once its aim, its strife — yes its wish — do attain proportions entirely beyond the scale of earth. But such aims, such strife for fuller completeness — though indeed we wish for them — are not mere wishes. They are part of the greater order of the world, which guarantees itself through the measureless past that felt no meaning in it, and surely is not now to stop just as we begin to see and share its meaning.

As Tennyson has said — who is the very poet of the larger hope : —

> "'Death's true name—
> " Is onward; no discordance in the roll
> " And march of that eternal harmony
> " Whereto the worlds beat time."

We know not how it is to be, or where. But somehow, somewhere, whether we wish for it or not, we know, by the dumb craving of the ordered world, as well as by the uttered hope of holiest souls that God will yet fulfill us into something better than the fragments that we are. And so we wait, and work and watch and do the best we may, or bow our heads in sorrow that our doing is so much below our best — and as His laws ordain we let life go, or fall asleep, but always for some further greater life beyond the shadows and the sleeping.

THE NEARNESS AND REALITY OF THE HEAVENLY WORLD

THE " Heavenly World." We want to have a happier and more realistic thought about it. Why is it, that while the belief in living again is so universal and deep-rooted that it seems impossible for our race ever to get away from it, yet the actual thought of that life to come, is, to most people utterly vague, shadowy and unsubstantial? I do not think that Life to come is what it might be to us. Yet, in the present day, especially, when all the difficulties about Immortality have been faced and investigated as never before, and found to have nothing really in them, it seems such a pity for us not to have all the help, and inspiration, and rest which this great thought, legitimately viewed, has in it.

I speak of this great thought " legitimately viewed " For when I come to consider why it is, that with such general belief that it must be, there is so little happy, realizing faith in it, I am convinced that it very largely arises from not viewing it legitimately, from thinking about it on a wrong line, from trying to form our conceptions of it in precisely the wrong way.

See; the trouble is, in this idea that possesses the common mind that the Heavenly World is something much less real and actual than this world. But how comes this idea? Chiefly, I believe, from this wrong way of thinking: — from trying to attain a conception of the higher spiritual life and spiritual world by contrast with this, and negation of this. People draw a broad contrast between body and soul, between material and spiritual. They strip away from their thought everything associated with bodily existence, and take it for granted that the remainder will be the spiritual. Everything material is exhausted out of their conceptions, or only used to indicate what the spiritual is not. Well, what comes of that? simply a list of negations. Spiritual things and the spiritual world are not this, and that and the other. They are not solid, they are not liquid, they are not even æriform; they have not shape, or color, or weight, or anything else that material substances have, and so the whole idea of the spiritual world is gradually reduced to something shadowy and spectral, something as near nothingness as possible. Is it surprising that with such an idea — or rather such a lack of any idea — people find it rather a dismal prospect? Is it surprising that they really feel — though they may be afraid to say so, lest it should sound irreligious — that they very much prefer the present? I do not wonder at it. For with all its drawbacks the present is a glorious world! There is a genial warmth in its sunshine, a wholesome bracing in its very cold. Its fields shine with a pleasant green; its good things are most unmistakable realities, and the grasp of a friend's hand is a substantial joy, compared to which there is something very vague and unsatisfying in a life in which people are almost afraid to count upon even knowing each other.

But now, I ask why should this idea of the shadowy, spectral unreality of the Heavenly World exist? The whole process by which men come to it is a wrong one. This plan, of exhausting out all that seems most real from our present existence, in order to conceive the spiritual, is a mere throwing away of the very helps to thought which Nature gives. The truth is, and all science and all philosophy are now tending to this, that we ought just to reverse this course. Whatever that may really be which we call the spiritual, the way to some living apprehension of it, is, by looking at material things not as its opposites and contrasts, but as its likenesses and types, and perhaps even its beginnings only in a lower realm. From height to height climb the realities in this vast universe of being; and from those we see, to those we cannot see, must be still the same orderly path. And even science is helping us in this. For it is not only shewing us this steady upward trend and drift of things; but it is shewing us how, even in the mere material universe, the most tremendous factors are not the visible substances, but elements and forces only perceptible at all by their effects, and as impalpable to any outward sense as Soul and God. So Science, and the Philosophy which grows out of it, are really helping us to the conclusion that whatever matter and spirit really are, it is spirit and the spiritual element in Being which are the most real, and the most enduring realities of all. So the legitimate way of thinking about the spiritual world, is not by stripping away from our thought of that world the elements which give the impression of reality, but by using them — as hints and suggestions — and thinking along the line of them, only beyond them to something more intensely real and glorious.

I am confirmed in this way of thinking towards Heavenly things, by finding that this is just the way in which those have thought, and shaped out their thoughts who have most lived in the Spiritual life, and whose thinking and seeing have reached furthest into those higher realms of being. I do not take these words of Christ and Paul as cut and dry revelations. They are not substitutes for our thinking, but helps to it, helps to show us the direction in which to think, and to make us sure that, in that direction, lie the great realities of God and Heaven. And see — every one of these great Words of theirs is alive with these two thoughts for which I am pleading — of the nearness and reality of the Heavenly World, with earthly things used as helps towards apprehending it!

Look first at that idea of nearness. Almost every allusion to Immortal life in the New Testament shows how near they felt it a Heavenly World only separated from this by what Sears calls " a thin partition of unconsciousness " In that clear thought of Christ, the immortal life is already begun. " This is life-eternal " he says — speaking of the higher life of men now; — and, " not dead but sleeping " is the continual word in which he utterly refused to treat what men call dying as such an utter, hopeless end of earthly love. All this was more striking then, than it seems now, because the Jews

thought only of some infinitely distant resurrection day, and that, until then, the dead remained unconscious or mere ghosts in the dim,
gloomy underworld. How different Christ's
feeling about the Heavenly World! You see in
his whole life and spirit the tokens of a sense
of that Heavenly World as close about him; now
and again its presence is felt so vividly that it is
as if its very glory shone out into the lower
visible world, — as at his Baptism and in the
Transfiguration. So, in his language when he
is about to leave them. It is the language of
one going away but not far — " to prepare a
place for you " he says — where they would soon
be with him again. I can think of no better
word to express it, than that I have already
quoted — of a world separated from this not by
some great interval of time or space, but by " a
thin partition of unconsciousness." Unconsciousness on this side only; " A little while and
ye shall not see me "; but, he says, " I am with
you even to the end of the world "; and again
" There is joy in the presence of the angels of
God over one sinner that repenteth." This was
Christ's habitual thought, and this was the
thought of the Heavenly life which the Apostles
learned of him. They believed that this was
specially brought home to them by his Reap

pearances, — that in some strange way, when they, after the thought of their time, supposed him dead until some far off resurrection-day, he appeared to them, shewed them that he was already risen, and made that Heavenly World in which he was, a different thing to them from what they had ever dreamed of before! Before, they had believed in a dim far-off Future state — now they felt it as a glorious Heavenly World, where Christ was and the saints. This is the meaning of that glad watchword of the early church — "Christ is Risen," it was not the re-iteration of his having reappeared to them, it was the ever renewed affirmation of that present Heaven which his reappearing from it had made so intensely near to them. There he was alive for ever more, still their master, loving, patient, — watching them in their service, making inter-cession for them in their weakness, waiting to welcome them to his own place. Stephen dying, sees Heaven opened, as earth's light grows dim, and cries "Lord Jesus, receive my soul!" The living and the departed are, in their thought, only "one family in earth and Heaven." And so, all through, you feel how present and close at hand they felt the Heavenly World to be, — scarcely divided from this world, and lying close beyond the shadowy gates of death, through which its dawning splendours often broke upon the just departing soul.

And, again, — they thought of the Heavenly world not only as close at hand, but, as intensely real. I spoke just now, of how, in trying to come at some idea of man's immortal state, we are apt to begin by stripping away from our thought of it, everything visible and tangible — everything that specially impresses the feeling of reality, in the present existence. Now it is noticeable that they took exactly the opposite way. I do not mean that they carefully reasoned it out just so; — simply, that in their endeavour to shadow forth those spiritual realities which had become so much to them, they gladly used the realities of the present. That is the meaning of Paul's reiteration, in many forms, of the idea of a "bodily resurrection." He does not mean that these earthly bodies were to be raised up again — that is the clumsy misunderstanding of his words in later and grosser times. He himself distinctly repudiates the idea of any such revivifying of these bodies. "Flesh and blood" he says "cannot inherit the Kingdom of Heaven." "Corruption does not inherit incorruption"; — mere physical substance has no place in that realm of spiritual existence to which soul belongs. Yet, "It is sown a natural body,

it is raised a spiritual body." What that
" spiritual body " is to be, and what the nature
of that glorified world in which it is to be, he
says nothing; there was nothing to say — " it
hath not entered into the heart of man to conceive the things which God hath prepared for
them that love him." Only — it is all *real,*
he says — not merely spectral, as people thought
before, and many fancy now, — not shadowy
phantoms in a phantom state. He is laboring,
all the time, to bring out the thought of how that
is the real world, and its things the absolute
realities, while this, though real, too, after a
poorer, temporary fashion, is, by comparison at
least, changeable, fleeting and evanescent!

It is this thought, the sense of how this was
the way in which they used the sense of earthly
reality to help the perception of the reality in
Heavenly things, — which gives us some opening into the real meaning of that curious book
of the Revelation. You have, in that book, the
visions of one of the devoutest minds of that
first age — caught up in his communion with the
Divine spirit into the intenser sense of Heavenly
realities, seeing, as in mighty sweeps of light and
glory, the collapse of the giant powers and
wrongs of earth, and the triumph of God's Will,
and the rejoicings of the Saints, and the final

merging of all poor earthly things into the glories of the new Heavens and earth! Some people are repelled by its strong material imagery; they smile at those quaint reiterations of gold and gems and precious stones, — emeralds and pearls and sapphires; — but as I read them, the impression they produce is this: of a mind filled with great thoughts and glorious images, groping round and round among the brightest and most glittering earthly splendours, in the effort to find any words and images by which he might convey to others some imagining of the unspeakable things of God. Will you "pooh, pooh," it all, as exaggeration? It is just the other way! short of the truth, not beyond it, — poor, imperfect, like the tawdry pictures of some grand scripture-story that one used to see upon cottage-walls, — yes, and yet, like such rude pictures, giving to our poor earthly minds craving for something real, some dim yet glittering image of the glorious world to come.

You see I have not attempted to claim for scripture any formal authority, nor to use it in any close literalism, as giving any exact descriptions of heavenly things. But I do feel it a mighty help in making us sure that the unseen things are real, and in encouraging us to think towards them with more realistic thought. Even Nature, at its lowest makes it impossible to believe that death ends all, but that is about as far as Nature goes. It does not give any glad happy sense of real life to come. For that we have to go to these great Masters of the spiritual life — they may be only a part of Nature, still, but Nature, then, at its highest. And as we go to them — to this great Christ, and those who came nearest to his thought, and put our hands in theirs to walk with them, they at least make us feel that the Heavenly things are real, not phantoms, or shadows. They do not give us finished pictures of the Heavenly world. That is what we are not to have here. But what we want to have, and what we may have, is, a glad assurance that — though we cannot think it all out, it is not less real than we can think, but more!

And therefore, too, I love the Easter-time, which brings to us again its great words and tones of realizing faith, born of that older time. It is good for us to sing those old songs — of the Heavenly World, and of Christ being risen there, and of the Angel-hallelujahs, and the light that has no fading! I know that these are, all, above the sober levels of experience. But that is the very reason we want them — to remind us that these sober facts of earth are not all, are only the least of all that is; to help us to feel that the Heavenly world is near and real; and that the world we see, real as it is in its own lower order of existence, is but like a shadow or a dream compared to the infinitely brighter and more glorious reality of the world we cannot see.

Do you ask — how may all this be? How can there be another world, more real than this, close to us, round about us ever, and we unconscious of it? Thinking how this might be, and how I might make it plain, an illustration recurs to me, used by one of those writers I have referred to — an illustration which some of you may have met before, but which will well bear repeating.

Suppose a little child fallen asleep amid summer scenery. In that sleep, the child is shut into a dream-world of his own. In that dream-world he sees pleasant and beautiful things; he plays with his dream companions, gathers the flowers, plashes in the stream — and so happy is he that his cheeks are aglow, and a smile plays upon his lips. It is all real to him, — and for the time he knows of no other existence. Yet all the while he is in a world still more bright, infinitely more real, and he has not the faintest consciousness of it! The fragrance of actual flowers is wafted over him, and he does not perceive it; the actual music of the birds sounds sweetly, but he does not hear it. Now, mark; the child is in two worlds at once — consciously in the one, unconsciously in the other. How will you transfer his conscious living from the first, to the last? How will you bring him from the dream-land into the real world? Not by taking him a journey through space, but simply by waking him up. What a change is there then! For a moment a confused, half-painful sense of the things amid which he has been so happy fading from him, but then in a moment more the joyful perception of the real world into which he has so strangely passed.

So, do I sometimes think it may be, in the passing from our present earthly existence into that greater life in which this present shall by and by be swallowed up. I know that no earthly similitudes can adequately figure forth these deep and wonderful things — but if they can even help us to some stronger clearer thought, let us not despise them! And after all, compared to that greater life, this little span of earthly years is only like a dream! Compared to its imperishable realities, these objects of earth that are silently changing every moment, are but as the shadows which fill our dreams.

Like the little dreaming-child we think there can be nothing so real; but the watching angels must smile to see the eager expressions of passion, hope, and fear, which pass over our faces. And in a little while the Father-presence bending over us will touch us with that kind hand which in our blindness we call the hand of death — and even while the visions of this earthly life fade from us like our dreams, the glorious realities of the Heavenly world will open to our changed and wondering sight!

THE INSPIRATIONS OF SCIENCE

I WANT my closing word in this volume to be on the confirmation and even inspiration which Science in its later stages is giving to all the upward reaching thought of man, and especially to his religious faith and feeling. When I was beginning my ministry, the talk was all about the difficulties and perplexities of Science. And indeed they were very real. The material world was being explored in every branch of it with such brilliant realism that the spiritual world seemed vague and doubtful in comparison. The difficulties touched the whole circle of faith — the thought of God — of any soul in man — of immortality; even of any divine authoritativeness in morals — so that many people lost much confidence in that side of life, in all the study and exercise of religion. It seemed to lack reality compared with the exact investigations of outward and tangible nature. I have felt all that myself. One does not need to be a scientist to follow with intense appreciation what the scientists are doing and thinking. Why, there were years in my earlier work when hardly a three months passed without bringing some new step of discovery, or some new forecast of theory by those who seemed to see and think the furthest, which made one feel anew as if the whole underpinning of religion and worship was being knocked away. And there could be no evading it — at least for churches that had fairly planted themselves on freedom and thought. I once heard Oliver Wendell Holmes say that "alone among Christian Churches, Unitarians had faced the modern discoveries of science with perfectly open eyes." And of course that meant perplexity and doubt for a time.

But now we are going to have our reward! For if one does not need to be a scientist to feel the difficulties science presents, certainly one does not need to be a scientist to appreciate its affirmations and even its inspirations. And it has come to me of late that really taken altogether, its great new discoveries not only do not touch the ancient reverence of mankind, but in their larger, broader sweep of meaning set it upon a firmer base, and with an infinitely higher reach of meaning.

The first of these inspirations of science that

I will speak of is the reassurance of the Eternal Goodness which has come in the fuller unfolding of Evolution. At first you know, Evolution seemed to bring insurmountable difficulty to religious faith. As men traced it working here and there, they seemed to find everything silently doing itself by impassive law; no place for God and certainly no place for divine goodness. The law seemed not only impassive but merciless: that "struggle for existence" with the weaker always going to the wall, filling the world with strife and cruelty: a thousand things in nature and in history which no ingenuity of reasoning could show in any light of goodness. No! but gradually as the whole scope and immensity of the great thought of Evolution has appeared, — as daring, sure-footed thinkers have traced it, back and back through the vast periods that geology proves, and that astronomy has to infer, there has risen up the sense of an ordered meaning, present through the whole, which awes the mind. Even in the passing detail — as of some gracious beauty in a flower or the curious wonder of an insect spinning a cocoon, one is constantly touched by an irresistible impression that something means this; but when you glance along the whole vast cosmic process this sense of a mighty meaning becomes almost over-

whelming. When the astronomer takes me
back to the primal fire-mists for the remotest
beginnings of worlds, and shows me those fire-
mists circling into spheres and systems, and
some cooling into globes; and at last a strange
new element of life appearing, covering the
globe with verdure, coming at length to animal
life, at first in lowest forms, but through the
measureless periods developing into higher forms
of infinite variety — from monad into mammal,
and up to man; and all things coming at last to
the infinitely varied wonder and beauty of the
world as we see it about us to-day — why; simply I may shut my eyes, just dazed, and refuse
to think about it at all; but if I do think about
it, I cannot help recognizing in it all, thought,
meaning — orderly meaning, and progressive
meaning.

This is something of an inspiration, this reassurance of an eternal meaning, that we at
least are not chance atoms, drifting like floating
specks of foam upon a tideless ocean dense with
mist — but parts of a vast, traceable, onward
movement — a movement that has already come
to wonderful things, and touches us with an irresistible sense of further meaning still.

And not meaning only. I think it comes to
us, in this longer look which Evolution gives,

that it is a good meaning, that the power which dominates the whole must surely be good. We may not see it in the passing event. You watch things as they are working out to-day, and there is much to cause doubt as to whether the power which causes, or even permits it, can be good. Books have been written on the cruelty of Nature. " Red in tooth and claw " as Tennyson writes, a " scene of incessant strife " as Huxley called it. That " struggle for existence " — all things preying on one another, has an awfully merciless look, as if some vast machine were just tearing things to pieces — living things to pieces — all the time. And when you look into the human world, it does not need Dahomey and its horrors; life on the underside of civilization; East-end life in hard times; plague or famine among the close-packed millions of India — how our hearts shudder for such things and long for some tiny scrap of omnipotence, to make them less. And sometimes things culminate in such crises of agony — such agony as Alva's soldiers wrought in Holland three hundred years ago; such agony as Armenia has suffered in our very sight; such sharp points of unutterable horror as that crowding, trampling multitude at the Moscow Coronation or that fiery furnace at the Paris Charity Fair — that one feels like shrieking out against any idea of goodness in God, if God there be.

I know! I have felt all that! But still, what is it makes us horror-struck at such things? What is this pity that we feel? Whence comes it? This also is part of this long process of Evolution. It seems a curious thing, does it not, that this slow, silent, working of things together which has brought the world on even by all this struggle for existence has, as its finest result, evolved a Being capable of looking into the struggling process and criticising it, and being saddened by it, and trying to mitigate it? At the first flash of it, it seems as if there might be two processes of Evolution, one evolving nature higher and higher, but with these forces of struggle and merciless outcome of suffering; and the other evolving man, up to mercy and pity and help. But no! The whole is one vast complex process, and surely then, it is in this highest, latest product — man — that we have the real interpretation of the whole, that "to which the whole creation moves." Yes; there is plenty still that we do not understand; but such a steady unfolding, through such inconceivably vast time, of ordered meanings leading finally to man — man conscious of what goodness is, and loving it and feeling it the very greatest thing of all — that the whole grows upon me more and more, in spite of much I cannot understand, as a very inspiration of Faith in the Eternal Goodness — goodness the final meaning of the whole.

There is one of the inspirations of the great scientific truth of Evolution. Another is, the trust it gives us in the higher indications of our own nature. Here is this moral life in man, this which comes out in principles of righteousness, which makes laws and sets up the world's institutions of justice and struggles for the good. Here is man's religious life " feeling after God, if haply it may find Him " seeking for some life above man's self to worship and to lean upon in prayer and trust; and not only feeling after God but seeking after some further life to come. What is all this? And can man trust these things, as anything real, or are they mere restless and morbid fictions of man's conceit, taking the echoes of his own thought for intimations from a higher realm?

As this questioning age has tried to apply its science to these vague, immaterial things, they have seemed so vague, so intangible, so impossible of verification by any scientific process, that there has grown up a wide-spread scepticism about them, and all sorts of theories have been shaped out as to how they came — not only **to** be — but to prevail so widely among mankind. The thought of God has by some been traced back to the savage's ignorant dread of the powers of nature. The thought of further life to come had its beginning, we are told, in dreams. The sense of right and duty may have grown up out of the accumulated motives of self interest. And so all round the circle of man's out-reaching life towards the Infinite and the Divine, he has been beaten back, as it were, upon himself, and even Evolution itself has been pressed into the service to explain how such blundering aspirations may have arisen, and to marshall his retreat from the supposed cloud-land of superstitious fancy to the solid ground of facts.

Well, all that explaining away has been pro foundly unsatisfactory. Multitudes have felt their lives poorer for it, even while they have sorrowfully allowed that they could see no other way. Men and women have longed to pray, and felt the old songs of worship tremble on their lips, but have choked them down because they fancied science had shown only empty vastnesses of space, where once, they thought, was a listening, loving presence. It is all a blunder! Science has done nothing of the kind, and Evolution, when you take in **the** full vast meaning of it, does the very opposite! For Evolution has not only evolved plants and beasts, it has evolved man — and man not only in the physical frame in which you can still trace the continuous plan, but in higher faculties and powers and feelings which seem above all connection with that lower life of his evolved beginnings. As I try to contemplate what the evolution of Man means, my mind is filled with awe. Why, even the slow processes which have evolved the beauty of a flower or the prehensile power of the elephant's trunk — how wonderful it is to think of them. But think of the evolution of a *man*: the development of mind: the growth of the first rude tribal sense of right into the "categorical imperative" of a conscience; the evolution of animal lust into pure human love; all the higher range of human qualities which are the most tremendous forces in history — the passion for righteousness, the "enthusiasm of humanity," the up-look to some higher life than man's, the on-look to some further existence than the present. Even as mere phenomena of the present these things are too great, too uniform, too widespread, to be dismissed as mere curious variations of morbid growth. But when we take them in their place in this vast orderly evolution of human nature, why, their place is the

topmost and the surest place. "Evolution"
not only permits us so to view them, but com-
pels us to do so, unless our whole process of
thinking is to be put to confusion. Evolution
surely, guarantees its own best and permanent
results. Man is the meaning of the whole. The
Mind is the meaning of man; and among the
qualities of mind, surely those are the highest
in which he rises to the sense of duty and dares
to think of faith in God and in a further life to
come.

Consider this last thought for a moment, for
it is on this that thinking people have become
most confused and discouraged to-day, the question of life to come; and it is on this that any
large thought of Evolution seems to me to have
an absolute inspiration. Look at it as a mere
academic question of to-day, and there is a good
deal to be said on both sides. Certainly, the
further life has never been proved. No certain
voice comes to us across the void. The promptings of nature, as you and I may feel them to-
day, are vague and ill-defined. No one has
ever traced the vital spark beyond the body's
life, or even found it as anything distinct at all.
No! but just here, where all our observations of
to-day seem somehow to fail us, comes in the
significance of Evolution. Look at the thought

of further life in the long development of man. It is no tardy conclusion from fragmentary arguments, but part of the mighty chain of tendency. You trace something of it as long as you can trace man at all. Goldwin Smith has lately written one of the most trenchant criticisms of all the common arguments for life to come; but at the end he admits that " there does seem to be a voice in every man which, if he will listen to it, tells him that his account is not closed at death." He seems to regard this as only a slight concession, indeed; but really, in the light of this vast orderly Evolution, it carries the whole thing. What is it that puts in man those faint dim tendencies which keep pushing him on a little and a little more along those lines of character which lead on through incalculable ages from the savage to the sage and saint? It is not mere desire. Why, oftentimes this sense of further life has taken forms which have been a dread and made man long not to be. To use again that saying of Dr. Martineau's " Man does not believe in immortality because he has ever proved it; but he is for ever trying to prove it because he cannot help believing it." It is part of his evolution. And this great Nature, which does not evolve an instinct in the meanest insect without something to correspond to it, may we not trust it in the greatest thought which it has evolved in the heart of man?

And just here comes in one more of these Inspirations of Science. For see; all through man's thinking of what he has called " soul," of whether there is such a thing and of whether it is to live again, he has kept groping about among the resources and possibilities of the material body and the material world. Especially he has been hampered by the difficulty of conceiving of life not resident in and continued in some body. How shall this life of mine continue to be in this personal consciousness which alone would be any real immortality, if this material body through which it acts and feels, is simply dissolved and ended? I do not know; and once, that " I do not know " seemed a grave argument against any such continuity. But how is it to-day? Why, science itself has simply risen above all that apparatus of investigation and reasoning which used to feel limited by the resources of matter. Science itself has passed beyond materialism. In its finer researches to-day it is moving freely and confidently among elements which are just as indiscoverable by any direct perception as life or soul in man, or as God in nature. Its most fixed terms are turning out to be mere algebraic symbols. We do not even know what matter is, or whether it is any real thing, or merely a succession of ideas or impressions such as we have in dreams, which yet seem so real. This electricity, what is it — of which no one can say whether it is a substance or a force? This ether, which no eye has ever seen, nor finest instruments detected its presence, and yet which scientists are agreed must exist, pervading even the mass of steel or stone, among the particles like air among the separate lumps in a coal heap, and equally filling the vast interstellar spaces? Or these "X Rays" own ing in their very name how utterly beyond all previous conception they are? Life? What difficulty can there be about life or life's continuance when all thought of the mere body and of matter and substance together, is widened out by facts like these? Once be sure that life is, at all — that you and I are points of conscious life — and that "conscious life" is the most wonderful and most tremendous thing in the Universe, and there is no difficulty about its continuance, if its own mysterious nature and tendency seem to point that way.

Ah, no! The real, greatest wonder is not how personal life should continue, but how it ever came to be. But having come to be, and having evolved into this consciousness of self

and ability to look into the universe and into itself; and all the way impelled towards goodness
and towards the worship of some higher power,
let us tread confidently on, sure that this Universe is verily the expression of that higher
power and is not going to land us in chaos or
intellectual confusion.

Even Paul, in that old time when men had
spelled their way into so little of the universe,
thought that enough was seen for men to glorify
the invisible power and Divinity: " The invisible
things of Him from the creation of the world
are clearly seen, being understood by the things
which are made." How much more so now!
This is the inspiration with all this wonderful
science of our time enriches and clears my mind.
It lifts me clear out of the half-meaning and confusion of the moment to a great height, from
which I see the whole creation ever moving on,
in orderly growth, even the mere earth coming
ever to a nobler type; and the creatures that
somehow grew up in it developing through awful
silences of time from beast to man; and man
growing from man the savage into man the
thinker, and growing still in conscience, affection, worship, faith; and ever, part of that faith,
the looking on to greater life still beyond. And
then just when such soaring thought seemed

blocked and contradicted by the poor limitations of the body and the earth, science rends the veil, shows us the dull, hard, matter that seemed to hold us prisoners, as a mere ethereal texture, free to all the purposes of God and for whatever may be his uses and destinies for man.

Yes, these are inspirations, inspirations to man to lift himself up from the ground; to trust his higher nature, and, even in the commonest lot in which he has to live, to walk with a great faith in God, and a great up-reaching heart of wondering adoration.

Lightning Source UK Ltd.
Milton Keynes UK
UKOW06f2048280816

281690UK00007B/388/P